PRAISE

"An accessible, lyrical pathworking [...] Year with Byron as your guide. There are few of us so lucky as to have someone to hold a lantern on the wild way of returning to ourselves and to the animistic heart of the Goddess traditions and the Old Ways. A beautiful ode to personal gnosis and self-trust."
—**REBECCA BEYER,** author of *Wild Witchcraft* and *Mountain Magic*

"Through this book, you will take a year-long journey both without and within. … Spiritual, magical, and completely original, this is one you don't want to miss."
—**DEBORAH BLAKE,** author of *The Eclectic Witch's Book of Shadows*

"This book reads like a giant embrace from the arms of the Goddess Herself. You will feel Her love—and dare I say Appalachian hospitality—on every page."
—**TRISTA HENDREN,** author, editor of *Girl God Books*

"Each meditative journey explores the wild and untamed aspects of the Goddess and oneself. The book brims with Ballard's unique wisdom and picturesque storytelling, challenging readers to step out of their comfort zones and into the cauldron of the ancient feminine."
—**MAT AURYN,** author of *Psychic Witch*, *Mastering Magick*, and *The Psychic Art of Tarot*

"A transformative journey that encourages readers to delve deep into themselves and uncover hidden aspects of their being. Through its pages, you will embark on a path of self-discovery, exploring the interconnectedness that binds us all."
—**JEN SANKEY,** author/creator of *Enchanted Forest Felines Tarot* and *Stardust Wanderer Tarot*

"The most empowering work I've ever read.... [It's] a journey that will lead you to places both familiar and unknown—some lush and nurturing, others wild and terrifying.... It is definitely a must-read for every woman on the planet!"
—**DOROTHY MORRISON,** author of *The Craft* and *Utterly Wicked*

"An intense work by a proven guide to the otherworlds that exist right here alongside our own. This book doesn't stay on the page; it follows you into your dreams."
—**ANGIE BUCHANAN,** senior minister and spiritual director of Earth Traditions and Gaia's Womb

"Through this primal and redemptive pilgrimage, we shed layers of domesticated frozenness and begin to remember the warmth, scent, and pleasure of our aliveness.... Byron offers us a lamp, a map, and a knapsack of nourishment, and she sends us off into the Wilds to reclaim our souls and rebirth a world of visceral relationship with all that is."
—**ERYN SCHRADER,** host of the *Plant Witch* podcast

"A heartfelt and richly imaginative collection of journeys to take you into the heart of the Goddess and deeper into yourself. Every part of this book sings and speaks to the author's profound depth of purpose and vision."
—LEVI ROWLAND, author of *Mother: Ecstasy, Transformation, and the Great Goddess*

"A beautifully written sacred journey.... The author tenderly holds the visions of the Divine Feminine through the different representations of Her in various faith and spiritual traditions.... *A Feral Church* calls us to rethink the feminine divine and wake up to her messages radiating around us."
—REV. JERRIE HILDEBRAND, Circle Sanctuary minister and President Emerita of the Covenant of Unitarian Universalist Pagans

"*A Feral Church* is essential work.... It is a text that will passionately and purposefully work you into a deeper understanding of the crossroads at which we stand while illuminating the hope and imagination needed to reenergize the feral churches in our own communities."
—PATRICIA BALLENTINE, priestess, artist, and writer

"Ballard explores the questions and experiences that may help center our minds.... On this journey, some will make it back to their new home and others won't. But for all who have gone before, they will leave breadcrumbs to find Terra Mater, or Mother World. This book is one of those breadcrumbs."
—CONSTANCE TIPPETT, artist, creator of Goddess Timeline and Image of the Goddess

"From our backyards, out through the untamed wilderness, and into the wild, feral Unknown Lands, Byron guides us into personal encounters with the Goddess, the feminine divine. These journeys take place beyond any intellectual or academic understanding we may have of the Goddess archetype into raw, real experiences."
—**DIOTIMA MANTINEIA**, founder of Urania's Well Astrology and author of *Touch the Earth, Kiss the Sky*

"Byron nudges us to feel the magic in the most mundane, in the stories, lore, mythology and archetypes. Here her journey relates us all to the power and perception of Her, the divine feminine. ... Byron beautifully describes the timelessness in our world as we ourselves navigate the journey of life."
—**TANJA BARA**, writer, teacher, *Tanja's Shadow and Light*

"The Goddess book for the twenty-first century. Through the exquisite narrative of Byron Ballard, we find ourselves immersed in a journey into Goddess and nature."
—**REV. LAURA GONZÁLEZ**, priestess, minister, and host of the podcast *Lunatic Mondays*

"Ballard is uniquely and distinctly qualified to give birth to this prophetic book of theology. ...We do not so much arrive as we are transformed to the untamed, the unpredictable, and the practiced powerful."
—**REV. SARA SCRUGGS**, writer, pastor at UMC

"Ballard gives us a series of meditations that take us on a journey like no other. This book is a cross between fairy tale and history, rooted in both simultaneously, with real meaning for today's world. It's a sermon without being preachy. It's female to female, human to human, kindly delivered but pulling no punches.... It is, frankly, nonfiction at its finest."
—**CHRISTINE ASHWORTH,** author of *Scott Cunningham: The Path Taken*

"This is not a book of spells, rituals, or philosophical essays. It is a pilgrimage, not to a destination but into the ever new and ever old turning cycle of seasons and the reasons of life and the deepest places of the soul.... It is a deeply personal book and the author's mind, heart, and divine spark are unveiled and fully present."
—**IVO DOMINGUEZ, JR.,** teacher, author, and Pagan organizer

"With her gorgeous prose and pragmatic theological reflections, Ballard offers us a way through uncharted territory: not a map with 'X marks the spot' but a practice of becoming.... *A Feral Church* is at once comforting and challenging, and it may just be the tool we need to smash through layers of oppression to find liberation for all."
—**REV. LISA BOVEE-KEMPER,** Interim Minister, UU Community of Charlotte (NC)

A Feral Church

ABOUT THE AUTHOR

H. Byron Ballard holds a BA and an MFA in theatre arts and is a western North Carolina native, teacher, folklorist, and writer. She has served as a featured speaker and teacher at Appalachian Studies Association, Conference on Current Pagan Studies, FaerieCon, Florida Pagan Gathering, Gaia's Womb, ConVocation, Hexfest, Pagan Spirit Gathering, Pagan Unity Festival, Sacred Feminine Rising, Sacred Space, Scottish Pagan Federation, Sisters Rising, Starwood, Trees of Avalon, and others. She is senior priestess and cofounder of Mother Grove Goddess Temple and the Coalition of Earth Religions for Eduction and Support (CERES), both in Asheville, NC.

Her essays are featured in several anthologies, and she writes a regular column on croning for *SageWoman* magazine. Her books include *Staubs and Ditchwater* (2012), *Asfidity and Mad-Stones* (2015), *Embracing Willendorf* (2017), *Earth Works* (2018), *Roots, Branches & Spirits* (2021), *Seasons of a Magical Life* (2021), and *Small Magics* (2023). *The Ragged Wound: Tending the Soul of Appalachia* is her current work-in-progress, as well as a cookbook from Wyrd Mountain and a musical adaptation *of A Midsummer Night's Dream*. She also podcasts on Appalachian folkways and living as one of the *Wyrd Mountain Gals*.

Visit www.myvillagewitch.com.

A FERAL CHURCH

A Guided Journey to Find Magic,
Kinship & the Goddess

H. BYRON BALLARD

WOODBURY, MINNESOTA

A Feral Church: A Guided Journey to Find Magic, Kinship & the Goddess Copyright © 2025 by H. Byron Ballard. All rights reserved. No part of this book may be used or reproduced in any manner whatsoever, including internet usage, without written permission from Llewellyn Worldwide Ltd., except in the case of brief quotations embodied in critical articles and reviews.

FIRST EDITION
First Printing, 2025

Cover design by Shannon McKuhen

Llewellyn Publications is a registered trademark of Llewellyn Worldwide Ltd.

Library of Congress Cataloging-in-Publication Data (Pending)
ISBN: 978-0-7387-7636-1

Llewellyn Worldwide Ltd. does not participate in, endorse, or have any authority or responsibility concerning private business transactions between our authors and the public.

All mail addressed to the author is forwarded but the publisher cannot, unless specifically instructed by the author, give out an address or phone number.

Any internet references contained in this work are current at publication time, but the publisher cannot guarantee that a specific location will continue to be maintained. Please refer to the publisher's website for links to authors' websites and other sources.

Llewellyn Publications
A Division of Llewellyn Worldwide Ltd.
2143 Wooddale Drive
Woodbury, MN 55125-2989
www.llewellyn.com

Printed in the United States of America

Also by H. Byron Ballard

Asfidity and Mad-Stones (2015)

Earth Works (2018)

Embracing Willendorf (2017)

Roots, Branches & Spirits (2021)

Seasons of a Magical Life (2021)

Small Magics (2023)

Staubs and Ditchwater (2012)

Acknowledgments

I write my books longhand in a notebook. There is a page where I jot down the names of people who have helped or inspired me along the way—if I left that job until the books were finished, my memory would fail me and I'd leave out some very important people. I've thought about the strict but kind teachers who helped me survive middle school—Mrs. Gilmore and Mrs. Gudger at Sand Hill. The organist at my grandmother's church was a consistent cheerleader and guide—I give thanks for the life, work, and friendship of Mary Glass. Thanks always to my family who understand why I'm not around: Joe (who always helps), Kat, Jeff, Sarah, Terry, and Patrick. Clever Sophia is my model for the Baby in the Hollow Hill (with thanks to Alicia and Corvin for creating such a fine child). The late lamented "bad cat" Rusty makes an appearance, thanks to his long-suffering companion, Patrick Covington. There are so many (mostly) women in the collective Goddess-honoring communities who remind me daily why we do this work. Here are a few: Kathy Jones, Trista Hendren of Girl God Books, Alice Rain and Carole Moon of Sisters Rising, Glenys Livingstone, Arlene Bailey, Angie Buchanan, Amelia Solesky and Phil Solesky, and the once-and-future Wise Women Helani Hopkins and Alex Karshner. Thanks also to the Circle of Council of Mother Grove Goddess Temple who keep the temple candles burning in my too-frequent absence. The team at Llewellyn: Heather Greene, Lauryn Heineman, Donna Burch-Brown, Shannon McKuhen, Markus Ironwood, and more. Colleagues across the country who delight me and sometimes keep me sane—Denise

Alvarado, the Earth Spirit Community, Carin Baskin, Ellen Sandberg, Laura González, Angie Buchanan, Drake Spaeth, Jerri Hildebrand, M. Macha NightMare/Aline O'Brien, Lisa and Michael Svencicki, the other Wyrd Mtn Gal Alicia Corbin Knighten and her mama, my colleague and occasional apprentice Zee Strawderman, her dog Poptart, Krista Chapman Green and Gina LaMonte for their heart-searing music, and David Southwell and the Hookland Guide for kenning the weirdness in the land. All these friends are the wind in my tattered sails, and I owe them what can never be repaid. If there is any confusion or any inadequacies, they are mine and mine alone.

Dedication

This book and my heart are dedicated to the Beloved Dead who walked with me throughout its writing. First and foremost, of course, is Carol P. Christ, priestess and scholar. With her stand Mark Dooley, Vanna Fox, Debbie Reese, chocolate-loving Penny Darata, Sinead O'Connor (who loved the BVM, too), shroud-maker Mareena Wright, and Brenda Dammann, founder of the Church of the Horse.

This book is also for all those who have quietly tended Her sacred flame and Her holy wells for so long, with little fanfare. Let the great pipes now sound for Her, and for all of you who walk and have walked this ancient, Moon-drenched road.

Contents

Prelude: Pathworking from the Hedges and Edges   xix

PART 1: THE GREENING
WINTER SOLSTICE TO SUMMER SOLSTICE   1

Chapter 1: A Dangerous but Necessary Journey   3
Chapter 2: Beyond Servitude: Into the Wilderness   13
Chapter 3: Life under Ice: Creating Our Mythic Story   25
Chapter 4: The Grasslands and the Womb   43
Chapter 5: Sand and Monsters   55
Chapter 6: Wild Women, Witches, Maenads   65
Chapter 7: Mother Nature   73
Chapter 8: Warrior. Lover. Lawgiver.   91

PART 2: THE DARKENING
SUMMER SOLSTICE TO WINTER SOLSTICE   105

Chapter 9: Eating the Apple   107
Chapter 10: Tea and Wisdom: The Bookshop of the Ancient Mothers   123
Chapter 11: Blood and Bone   133
Chapter 12: Dancing on the Corpse Road   145
Chapter 13: Sin-Eating and Benedictions   157
Chapter 14: Wenceslas and the Five of Pentacles   167
Chapter 15: Terra Mater, the Mother World   175
Chapter 16: The Mycelia Way   183
Chapter 17: Seven Nights before Solstice   191
Chapter 18: The Ceremonial Return: The Great Road at Avebury   201

Postlude   215
Appendix: Feral Resources   217
Recommended Reading   223

Prelude
PATHWORKING FROM THE HEDGES AND EDGES

The entirety of this book is a pathworking, a series of meditations that take us from one solstice to another and then on again to end where we began. A pathworking, if you are unfamiliar with the term, is a meditative journey and is a new name for an old practice, one that allows the pilgrim to travel to places real and imaginary, exterior and deeply interior, in order to experience knowledge, wisdom, or healing. This is also the technique I used to write the book. I chose a location for each journey, and through meditation, I went to that place and put us into that setting to see what we could experience of the Goddess and what we could learn about ourselves and the land with which we dwell.

Place by place, we will embark together on a spiritual pilgrimage, leaving behind those things we find comfortable—a warm home, a nourished body, deep friendships with kith and kindred—to seek out the true, the authentic, and an expression of the Divine that is both ancient and modern, many and one. You and I will travel far and wide to bond with the goddesses of the wildest of places, whether undomesticated wilderness or the confines of our weary hearts, trekking toward a gut understanding of Primal Mothers, of what is "the female Divine," of systems that are breaking away from the dying of the West and transforming into something completely new, based on concepts of birth, health, deep nurturing, love, and rebirth.

☽○☾

By our nature and personal histories, many of us tend things; we are caretakers. We care for the land and beings around us. We are parents and gardeners, teachers, and nurses. We are the ones who feel bound to tend communities, to calm tempers, to mend rifts. We weave, we mend, we tend. We make the ragged thing whole: we fuse together the shattered edges and hope the mending holds. Then we turn to the next rip.

There is an inexhaustible supply of broken pieces to glue together in a recognizable way. We have no sooner repaired this one than to have shards of another broken person, animal, or community dropped into our soft laps. Then we stitch or glue or reweave it into something like the wholeness it once maintained. It is never as good as new nor as durable as before, but it is workable, recognizable, and usable. Until the next bout of careless or loveless handling and it falls into our ample laps once again. With each repair, a little of our tending and tender souls—which are part of the glue that holds it all together—is lost.

In the following journeys, we will move away from the hedges that mark the boundaries of our small lives. We are going to the edges of what we know...and then moving out from there into what the old maps called *terra incognita*, the unknown lands, the outlaw lands. We will go together into the wide world in search of the Divine Mothers and Their feral churches. There are places that can teach us much as we drop the trapping of civilization.

We dwell in cultures that emphasize healing, being healers, making others whole. Many in our communities have a strong pull toward the idea of healing (traditional, pharmaceutical, and alternative). There are circles for healing, workshops, and private sessions with well-known healers, with shamans and holy folks. They may encourage a painful evaluation of our personal history, our traumas, and our shames. Myriad techniques are offered to get us past the difficulties and pain of our lives in order for us to move forward, to be successful, to find a partner or job satisfaction or happiness.

So many of us are broken by life and living, moving from workshop to private session as we strive to be better and healthier. But some questions haunt us as we change, as we peel off layers of culture and history. How long do I need to be careful with my spirit, tender with all I have been through? When will I be healed enough to move forward or deeper? When will I be strong enough to do the work I see all around me, work that needs doing, work I can do? For many of us, it comes down to a question that is impossible to answer in a general way: How much healing is enough?

When we realize that we can heal as we grow, that we don't have to put the rest of our rich lives on hold while we contemplate all this, that is when we realize we have come to terms with things that have tormented us and stymied us. We may gingerly prod our souls to consider different paths, to carry an emotional and spiritual first aid kit that will mend us as we go. At that point, we begin to look for a way to align ourselves with the profoundly spirit-filled world in which we dwell and to be in kinship with that world, for the good of all.

That is when we long for a world that is filled with and allied with the best of our limited species—nurturing, nourishment, creation and birth, joy in living. A culture not of death, which is where we find ourselves most days, but a culture that celebrates life in all its processes. For many people, this means remembering that there was once a time when the Primal Mothers were honored for Their life-giving and fecundity. When Goddesses were revered as symbols for all that life encompasses—birth, growing, tending, and death.

This is where we stand now, in much of Western culture.

This pilgrimage we are on is a strange and necessary one. Many people are feeling themselves drawn to the Sacred and Primal Goddess and visualize Her in many forms. There is hard polytheism, which posits noncorporeal beings that are not human nor ever were. Their lives have an effect on the world of humans, and they appear in our cultural and religious histories but are somewhat removed from us. Humans do not become goddesses, nor are they goddesses now. You might as well say we become cats through our spiritual work—though to work metaphysical and spiritual processes to become cats would be mighty tempting. In addition to this firm plurality of spiritual female Divines, there is the idea of a monotheistic and female Source of the Universe in its entirety, a matrix within which resides the male principle, which is likewise sacred but not divine in the same way. Still others see Goddess and Goddesses as archetypes that have come into being to inform and encourage humankind, especially the female part of that species. We may find it necessary to choose one of these, but it may be that not pigeonholing the Divines will actually give us a better chance to discover the nature of this obscured but necessary thing we call Goddess.

As with most things spiritual and magical, there is a luscious abundance of books, videos, and websites to choose from to find the information we seek. Older books may use language that is confusing or hurtful to modern ears, yet they are still often worth the mental translation necessary to absorb valuable information.

We seek a place where true connection to the Primal Mother—the Goddess or Goddesses—can happen. It is not only the place of connection, but also a place where we can be away from the combined centuries of patriarchy and doctrine that repress everything female—except for the bits that can be used sexually or commodified in some other way. In seeking and finding a feral church, we fulfill Virginia Woolf's desire for a room of our own, only this time the room is a place of wild worship, a place of willful abandon, deep communion, and freedom. Freedom. Freedom. Freedom.

With this grounding and history, we begin our pilgrimage, for time is fleeing ahead of us. You may choose to begin this book-long series of pathworkings by giving yourself a quiet place to read and comfortable clothes to wear. We will travel together from place to place and from experience to experience and will give ourselves time at the end of each journey to assess what our perceptions have been of the work, what we have learned, and how it has touched or changed us. Indulge yourself in these journeys.

Take the time to linger in the world of each journey, to feel all you can about the land and people you meet throughout. A paper journal at your side may be a helpful way to record impressions and feelings, even the unfolding memories that often rise unexpectedly. A notebook can hold words, fragments of sentences, drawings, and images cut from magazines or printed from internet sources. It can be a repository of the treasures found on these journeys.

These fragments will accumulate throughout our yearlong sojourn and may be useful as remembrances of the path that wends away behind us when we are seated in the authority of the Maternal Divines and the power of the Earth Herself.

Throughout, I have chosen to capitalize "She" and "Her" when referring to the Goddess, the Goddesses, the Divine Feminine, and female divinity. "She" is used as both singular and plural and capitalizing the pronoun is to set Her apart in the reader's mind. These words are merely symbols for an energy, a being, who defies a boxlike definition that fits all the circumstances and personalities that She encompasses and births.

As in many guided meditations, the locations may be actual locales, or they may live only in the deep places of folklore and memory. Feel free to take a break after each chapter and ponder what might come next. Take your time, whether it be much or little, and let the pathworking move you out from your domesticated world and into this search for a place of wild worship and joy, a feral church that is not bound by dogma or liturgy.

When we can pause, when we can stop in the midst of personal and cultural chaos, we reach a still point. In these moments we dwell in a timeless place of no pressure to achieve, to do. We have only to be, to exist in our bodies, to collect our breath, to acknowledge the kinship with all that is, whether in the present or in what we perceive as the past and the future.

Sshhh. Be still. Listen.

Everywhere you can hear it—a rustling, a long-held breath released, a grunt, a growl. The divine spirit that is Goddess and Goddesses, singular and plural, has crept back into the world and into our lives. This force—these forces—have been deliberately repressed, hidden away in plain sight, so that it all feels fresh and edgy, the way we like it. The way we think we like it. Truly, She never left us and has always been literally the ground beneath our feet, the food we eat, the air we breathe, all that we need. It is we who have kept Her at bay, doubting Her, doubting ourselves. But now we feel it as a return, as a rising, and we welcome Her as we refamiliarize ourselves with the Primal Mothers.

Elder, Mother, Sister, Child. For those who have held Her—in whatever shape Her guising took throughout the centuries—in their hearts and their sinews for so long, this rising into the consciousness of the world has not come a moment too soon. The return has come when it is needed most—and we welcome Her and welcome our journey into a Mother World.

Part 1

THE GREENING: WINTER SOLSTICE TO SUMMER SOLSTICE

In this thoroughly modern age, filled with electric cars and artificial intelligence, it is easy to lose sight of our human connection to the intricate cycles that weave their way into every moment of every day. Some refer to this cycle of seasons and ceremonies as the Wheel of the Year because the seasons arrive, play their part, and then move on, only to perpetually return. This is one of the reasons many people don't perceive time as linear. It tracks back around with complete regularity. Our human lives grow thin, as these circles revolve, so we also honor the rites that mark our personal seasons, from birth to death.

If we consider the placement of solstices, we observe that from one solstice to the next, we experience more light-filled parts of the day and from that solstice to the next, the dark part of the day steadily lengthens. Earth's two hemispheres experience these cycles at opposite times. When it is greening in the Southern Hemisphere, it is darkening in the north and vice versa.

These occurrences are natural and observable as Earth revolves on its axis and circles the star at the center of our solar system. It doesn't require dogma or faith. Every culture has wrapped these events in story and myth, but they require neither, as the mechanisms exist far beyond the tinkering and interference of humankind.

Throughout most (if not all) of human history, these points of dramatic change have been noted and honored through celebration and ceremony. Our distant ancestors observed and documented both solar and lunar patterns, the latter being more easily observed because of the Moon's effect on the great collections of global water in oceans and lakes.

Our search for this ancient and feral connection to the Goddess will take us to places familiar and unknown. This eternal longing for strong connection to the Primal Mothers—for true worship—begins at the dawn of the darkest day and wends inexorably to the same day a year hence. As the cycle naturally runs, we will continue our quest into the darkest of days, within and without.

The first section begins here and is dubbed "The Greening." Midway through the book, we will acknowledge the swift intake of breath, the subtle turning that sends us into the world of endarkenment. We will call that section, leading us through those inner and outer pathways, "The Darkening."

Chapter 1
A Dangerous but Necessary Journey

This book emerged from a single event, one that had as its backstory decades of study and veneration. Some of you will relate to that sense of destiny, some will come to understand it, and for some of you it will feel like an attack on some of your long-held beliefs about all sorts of things—the nature of the Divines, history, systemic and systematic oppression, the roles of women, and others I won't expect.

That is the nature of personal writing and also the nature of religious writing. Make no mistake—this is religious writing. This is part of a new wave of Goddess thealogy at a time when "Goddess" is used to describe everything from a razor for removing hair from women's legs to your best friend who has made some hard choices. *Thealogy* is the study of and reflections upon the nature of the Goddess. It comes from the Greek root *thea*, which means "goddess."

I was teaching at a summer festival—and occasionally dancing naked around a bonfire, as one does—when I read that author Carol Christ had died. It was difficult to take in. I didn't know her personally, but her writings had a profound effect on me as I was stretching my mind and my soul to understand the nature of the Divine in my world. My world at that time was Shakespeare and vocal training, and the sort of young adult poverty that most liberal arts majors experience. My unchurched upbringing had left an odd gap in my understanding of "god," and my animist leanings coupled with a headful of folklore and mythology had colored my view of that august being, or beings, that are called "god." A firm grounding in Greek and Roman mythology had also lent me the notion of a multiplicity of divine beings, surely more exciting than the peculiar Father/Son/Holy Spirit that dominated the religions of my friends and neighbors.

Her essay "Why Women Need the Goddess" offered a new place to stand, a place that made sense to me on a cellular level and launched me into study, into veneration, and finally to the priestesshood and the founding of a Goddess temple in my hometown.[1] Dr. Christ is one of the foremothers of an international women's spirituality movement that inspired me, and her death brought me up short.

---

1. Carol P. Christ, "Why Women Need the Goddess," in *Womanspirit Rising: A Feminist Reader on Religion*, ed. Carol P. Christ and Judith Plaskow (San Francisco: Harper and Row, 1979), 117–32.

I sat in my uncomfortable camp chair and cried, drinking strong coffee laced with Irish whisky. When a friend saw my distress, she sat with me, and the discussion that followed made me realize that my decades-long journey had been exactly that. I had moved from a generalized idea of "goddess" to an academic understanding of "the Goddess" to a visceral connection with an unknowable Mystery, grounded in the soil and stone of the land I inhabit and wrapped in the dull and ragged shawls of my female ancestral line.

That long road was set with circles. Circles of women. Encounter circles. Empowerment circles. Healing circles. We talked and wept and raged. We read Gerda Lerner and Marija Gimbutas. We read Starhawk and Luisah Teish. We learned about archetypes and blood mysteries. Then we grew older and there were careers and children. We grew older in the sure and certain knowledge that the war in Vietnam was over, safe abortion was legal, and birth control was fairly reliable and certainly available. We sang and whispered, "The Goddess is alive! Magic is afoot!" Our spiritual lives became less frantic and more settled. When we prayed, god was a she and liberal churches welcomed passionate "women's spirituality" groups. Other matters—civil rights, homelessness, global climate change—demanded our focus, our good attention. Our lives were busy, filled with money problems, health problems, and partner problems. We got fearful and careful, but neither guaranteed safety.

With a globe expanded onto our desks and into our bedrooms, we watched the children around us face things we could barely imagine. Our minds turned to those old and heady days when we knew we were riding a changing tide, creating a better world, when the Goddess was alive to us and for us. But this hyper-connected world began to dismantle the things we'd created. The good things. What little safety there had been was dissolving even as we were examining our privilege, our codependence, our culpability for the things we hadn't addressed and the people who had been left behind. The grief and guilt were palpable, are palpable.

Just as we had redefined the word "witch," we now returned "crone" to its rightful place, even embracing "hag" as the keeper of sacred wisdom and gateway to the ultimate Mystery. We expanded "Maiden-Mother-Crone" into a seductive web of women's passages, more subtle, fuller of possibilities for growth and creation. We fumbled with the old words. We called the terrible, top-down systems by their oldest name—patriarchy.

The world we lived in had changed somewhat. But most of us didn't take the next steps. We sat in those encounter groups. We read books and magazine articles. We discussed Eisler's concept of "power over" versus "power with." We strove to be empowered and pondered the uses of power. We stood, at last, in our power.

But we'd never learned to wield it.

Our knowledge of the Divine had expanded, and that expansion allowed more nuanced approaches to Goddess. Yet our lives were, for the most part, set into the same grooves as those of our mothers and our grandmothers before them.

Centuries of playing subordinate roles to our fathers, partners, and sons—as well as rulers, priests, and bosses—modeled for us the ways in which we didn't want power used. Our intuition told us again and again that there must be better ways to wield power: ways in which authority could be used to make the world better for all, not only the people with wealth and social status. But there were precious few role models for how it could be used, how power should be used. The Goddess spirituality work that began with the women of the seventies continues with new generations. Social media platforms are full of people (not only women) longing for the destruction of top-down hierarchical systems. Still the systems persist.

It is time to learn to wield power. This will require journeys that challenge and disturb, external pathways into the wild places of the world and internal ones into the wild places of our souls.

THE JOURNEY

There is a sturdy and potentially invasive plant called privet; *Ligustrum* is the botanical name. It is in the small tree/large shrub category of plants, with glossy evergreen leaves. Privet is often used in the boundary-marking hedges of suburbia because it isn't thorny and is easily trimmed into the obligatory box shape so beloved in that region, thrusting itself between paved driveways, where it catches stray balls and wheeled child-vehicles. It has a sweetly scented bloom that becomes tiny inedible berries in the fall. The berries stay in place and don't fall onto the tidy concrete drive.

It is a marker. Cats and dogs can wriggle through, birds can nest, any wild growth is quickly noticed and easily trimmed into submission. In the grand gardens of Europe, there are hedges older than my country. Even in the stately homes of Virginia, there are carefully tended hedgerows that are scanned by diligent gardeners, the sickly and non-thriving ones pulled out and replaced so there is never a break in the line, only a young plant that will quickly grow to fill the gap.

As we stroll these calm places, our feet crunching on the gravel paths, we feel the inherent protection and vitality of the sculptured landscape. All around us is manicured, contained, exquisite. We arrive at the center of a set of matching planting beds where a low fountain lies. The water gently laps against the marble edging, the sound restful and monotonous. There is, of course, a statue in the middle of this koi-filled pond. She wears a serene look. Her short tunic reveals strong legs, and the feet are clad in sturdy sandals. She holds a slim bow in one hand, and a quiver of arrows lies against her back.

We stand as motionless as the archer, taking in the sound of water and birdsong. The smell of damask rose strikes our nostrils and the gold of the fishes catches our attention. We sit at the edge of the pool, letting our fingers flick the water. We breathe, relaxing. We sigh. We are lulled into a sleepy place from which we resist moving. Our eyes close: our breathing is slow and deep.

The Goddess of This Land is here, soothing our brows, reminding us of the peace of well-tended places. There is a quietness that settles into us. The daylight softens, the sounds quiet. We feel protected and secure. The Lady of This Land drops Her hands onto our shoulders. Our hearts are filled to bursting in this moment. Nothing is remembered that is not sweet and peaceful, this gentle and profound escape from the workaday world. We rest. We sleep. We dream.

Our senses lulled, we are no longer completely aware of our surroundings. Those senses are turned inward, observing our inner lives, accepting the comforts so freely given. Indulging in safety, we are drunk with the domestication of security. All is well, all are safe. Because of this lethargy, this unawareness, we do not see the arrow drawn silently from the quiver. We likewise do not see the statue's head move, the face of the Goddess turning toward us, Her suddenly blue eyes narrowing against the glare of the westering sun. We are shocked to hear the tiniest sound—a sound like the toenails of a mouse on a kitchen countertop—an arrow nocking into a bow string. It is this sound that brings us back to the world around us, out of our reverie. We rise swiftly, as the arm draws the bow back. Hardly comprehending, we watch the bright eyes sight along the arrow's shaft. If we have any conscious thought at all, it is driven from our minds as the arrow flies true, its feathers unruffled in the still garden. It strikes home—splitting the skin, the flesh, the muscle and nicking the bone, slicing straight and true through our hearts.

There is another sound then, an escape of air from parted lips, a sound less of pain than of surprise and ecstasy. She has claimed us as only this wild creature can, by slaying us to the former comfort that bound us, dulled us, and shrank our souls to fit neatly in any hand except our own.

Too late now. These hearts are sliced open, sheared into strips like old beef liver. No way to protect it now. It stretches from our ruined chests and slips out, into the sunset, and the pain, and the world.

We will follow as best we can on the journey of the Fool card in tarot, of every fairytale child who enters the forest, on the escape from the land of enslavement and bondage. It is definitely not the hero's journey, for we need no heroes. It is a path with no path and a road with no name.

Perceptions

The concept of "the wild" and "the wilderness" holds a vivid place in the imagination. Too often, though, our preference is to look at photos of dramatic wild places or to drive through them to places with more human-focused comforts. Even those who choose to spend time in the wild—whether hiking, camping, or doing other recreational activities—go there for peace and solace, not to encounter the wild on its own terms.

Thanks to human greed and overreach, there is precious little true wilderness left in the world, and what is left remains only because it is too difficult to extract its resources (due to terrain or climate) or its resources have not yet been commodified in such a way that the profit is worth the expense.

Wilderness is a place of refuge, of privacy, of seclusion. Outlaws run to the wilderness to evade capture and punishment and outcasts to escape the interference of other humans. The natural balancing of life's systems—seed to plant, cub to adult, germination to rot—are played out in such places without the baleful glare of modern culture.

In this journey, we enter the wilderness within us and are weaving pathworkings into the wilderness of our imagination. The lands we visit are as real as our imagination, as are the dangers we will encounter. The wild then becomes our classroom and our proving ground.

Chapter 2
BEYOND SERVITUDE: INTO THE WILDERNESS

To search for a divine connection, to enter into an acknowledged kinship with the divinity of the natural world, requires each of us who desire that connection to take a hard look at our own domesticity. The daily rituals that allow us to do all that modern life requires can become prisons in which we are mired, trapped in the repetitious, workaday ceremonies that begin with waking and end before we reach deep sleep. Breaking through the societal and familiar must-do acts is one of the hardest parts of the process. We willingly came to domesticity as the adult way of walking in the world.

Whether you are literally parenting, tending your own aging parents, or functioning as the parent or grown-up at work, the burden of mothering can be heavy and onerous. The trappings of this slow domesticity have dulled us into complacency in an effort to simply get all the tasks done that adult lives seem to require.

There is much discussion around issues of mothers and mothering. Many people, especially women, carry terrible wounds inflicted by the woman who bore them, a woman bending under the weight of the misogyny that has threatened women for longer than we can count. Whether she is your best friend or your mortal enemy, the woman who gave birth to you has had an effect on your life and sense of worth, for better or worse. Adults sometimes look to others to provide the nurturing that was missing in childhood, hoping to fill a hole that is empty of anything but longing and pain.

There are so many reasons for this break in the connection. One is found in the hierarchical systems that relegate women to second-class status. These systems are everywhere—in religion, in education, in family support or lack of it, in family, and in government. Another reason is profoundly biological—in order to find an appropriate mating partner, a young female of any species may need to separate from the family of origin to keep the genetic pool diverse. Once the mating occurs, in nature and in many cultures, the young female returns to the older one for assistance in child-rearing.

It is hard to separate us from our mothers, and Western culture assures us that we need to be independent and stand in our own individuality, separating us from that means of support. One of the ways we can break the hold of patriarchal influences is to choose to understand the hardships our biological mothers also endured, to aim for understanding, for forgiveness if that is possible or necessary. Keeping women suspicious of the bond that nature has given us to ensure the survival of the young is one way these systems continue to oppress and control not only women but also the men with whom they have relationships.

THE JOURNEY

After years of disease and isolation, many of us wander through life as carefully as if we were stepping on butterflies or shards of glass. We have withdrawn our energy from the larger world with its strangers and its dysfunctional communities. We have drawn into ourselves while also drawing away from each other. Carefully, carefully. Never treading forward but always stepping back, stepping around, limping in an ever-narrowing circle until we stand alone, off-center, facing the void, the great emptiness. Nothing is felt within, nothing without. Our skins are dry and cracked, no longer responding to moisturizing love or gentle attention.

Then we stop. The mirrors we face are darkened, foxed with age and neglect. No timid candle flame teases us to peer in. We shrug and can no longer rally thought nor will. What is left in this dryness when desire itself has forsaken us? We can be blown to dust in the slightest breeze.

Undone. Unmoored.

Lost.

In the time between despair and dissolution, something causes us to raise our eyes. The dirty mirror stands lifeless and empty, but beyond it, unnoticed until now, is a flick of movement. We peer through crusting eyes, trying to see what is there, out of reach and nearly out of sight.

A shallow breath escapes our parted lips. The ragged pulse skips a beat. On the edge of a crooked branch, three young leaves are a-borning, swiftly budding to an unbearable greenness. One, two, three. The branch swells and is the bony crooked arm of a woman, older than time, broader than the night sky.

The leaves lie in her etched palm now—fat, moist, luscious. She holds them out to us in the same way she'd give a treat to a tired horse. She knows our fear, our exhaustion, and our aching need. We step out of the suffocating circle with tiny steps that are awkward and unbalanced.

Her fingers flex, beckoning. We draw another ragged breath, take another step. Less tentative now but not yet strong. Our own hands reach out, the tips of our fingers touch that outstretched palm. We take one of the leaves and touch its coolness to our lips, drinking in the moisture. The second leaf is sweeter, heavier, richer. We feel life returning to our desiccated guts, expanding the lungs, quickening the heart.

The arms and hands have filled out, fleshed out. When our fingers pinch up the third leaf, the flesh of the palm is soft, the skin elastic and warm. This leaf smells of compost, of roses, of rust, of death. It is intoxicating and delicious.

And we are alive, our limbs strengthening. The hand withdraws through the thorns and brambles of a thick hedge. It is a hedgerow out of a fairy tale, the sort of verdant boundary that keeps the good within and the danger without.

We shake our heads to clear the jumble of images and thoughts. We are good and we are safe within. Good and safe, contained by a dense growth of all the green of the great round earth. We reach out our own hands to touch, to explore, learning what we can about what contains us here in this gray, loud, and busy place. The thorns rip our flesh and we continue. The brambles scratch and bloody us and we cannot stop ourselves. There is more here than we have ever considered. Blood, pain, luminous greenness, vibrant but untouched life.

A face appears then, pushing through the green and the blood and the spiking, arching bramble canes. The face is neither old nor young. No, old and young, shifting as we watch. A shimmer and she is a serpent, hooded and deadly. A fog obscures our eyes and she is the rock face of a cliff in winter. The vines shake and she is your mother, your daughter, your granddam. Then a shoebill crane, then an eel, now an aconite blossom.

We close our eyes and through the blurring of sweat and blood, she is death and winter, bone and rot. With a shake of her skull, she bursts into the fire and gas of a supernova and we are knocked back, burnt, destroyed, no more.

All our parts rise and reassemble, no heart, no mind. Only soul and spirit and a yearning for a connection we can't express and don't know. With shaking bodies and shattered selves, our reconstructed beings shift and moan. We howl and keen, pulling the shards of our hungry souls into a raggedy whole.

The smell of honeysuckle and blood fills our nostrils. We press our bodies against the thorns and brambles and we begin to climb. Up and through, until we reach the impossible crest of the monstrous hedge and gaze into the wild places beyond. With no hope of mercy or grace, we begin the journey to the

Mother who bore us, the serpent, the aconite, the world, and the infinite stars.

We plant ourselves in an eldritch place that bears all the hallmarks of somewhere we have known, have visited long ago, or can go to at some future time. Our journey in this moment takes us to a church that is real, is historic, that opens its doors to seeker, to penitent, to wanderer. We think it is not our church, that it is not Her church, but we may be surprised by the caretakers who have held Her for so long, always in the face of Her erasure, Her diminishment, and Her potential loss. We are aware we will meet Her again and again in our sojourns. She will wear many faces, speak with many voices, wear a plethora of guises. She and They, Mother, Grandmother, Queen, Sister, Martyr, Warrior.

We are standing on the sidewalk on a sunny day in a small town. A tidy and well-kept garden holds a dozen rose bushes in many colors, healthy plants, blooming. Great wooden doors are firmly closed against our entry, but that is an illusion. The carved front doors only open for Mass and special ceremonies, like weddings and funerals. We find the side door is always open to welcome the stranger, to offer sanctuary and consolation. We linger at the roses and remark on the skill of whoever the gardener might be who tends them. They are dazzling in the sunlight. It is the perfect time of year for these hybrid tea roses—not too hot, just enough rain, space between each bush for good air flow. We bend to take in the scent and, thus fortified, we wander around to the side door and find it propped open. It is a small, plain door with little windows near the top. It must be closed in cold weather, but the priest or docent will be able to look out those windows to see who may be coming in.

We know the ways of old churches. The door takes us into the cool narthex, the small lobby that holds a rack full of pamphlets and a table with hand sanitizer and tissues. There is also a bowl of holy water beside the door into the nave where believers may bless themselves before entering into the main part of the church. This particular church is a basilica and is built along a specific plan.

Quietly, we slip past the water and into the empty nave. Against the back wall to our left is a stand with tealight candles arranged in rows. A metal box with a slit in the top encourages those who would light candles at this station to drop in a donation. One of us fishes into a pocket and drops some coins in, then kisses the bottom of the tealight before lighting it from another candle. *For our journey. And for Her.* We nod. Yes.

We walk boldly down the center aisle toward the main altar. The candlesticks and other paraphernalia glow in the soft light, and they are placed on a white cloth. Flowers stand in great vases, leftovers from a recent wedding. It is a marvelous sight. We turn before we reach the altar and venture into the small chapel on the left. This is the traditional Lady chapel, and it is the reason we have come to this place, this formal and organized church, emblem of the very power we wish to leave behind, and to break if we can.

The Lady in question is the Christian Mary, the Blessed Virgin and Mother of the Divine Savior-Child. She is *Theotokos*, God-Bearer. This place is Her chapel. The altar has burning candles, and above it hangs a glass candleholder in deep blue. There is one formal flower arrangement in the center, but the steps that go up to the altar are strewn with single flowers and small bouquets. There is a teddy bear there and photos of children who need protecting or children who have died and are now in the heavenly protection of Christ's Holy Mother.

Behind the altar, a life-size statue of Mother and Child is lit from behind and from below, giving us a sense of timeless and formal Divinity, presence but not power. Instead of that distant and not approachable blue and gold vision, our eyes are drawn down to the pictures on the steps, the single stems of roses, the zinnias that obviously came from someone's garden.

We take seats on the folding chairs in the front of the chapel, facing the steps and the skirts of the cloth that covers the altar. We can see the ends of the table legs: hairy animal paws with claws. Lions? Dogs? We rack our brains to think about the animals associated with Mary and only come up with doves. But we remember Julian of Norwich and her cat and decide that the Blessed Mary probably has a cat, too, for companionship and mouse control.

One of us begins a Hail Mary very softly, a leftover from some long-rejected Catholic upbringing. But these things we learn as children often stick with us, and this is a good place to let that out.

> *Hail, Mary, full of grace, the Lord is with thee. Blessed art thou amongst women and blessed is the fruit of thy womb, Jesus. Holy Mary, Mother of God, pray for us sinners now and at the hour of our death.*

There it is again. *Theotokos*. God-bearer. Not god. Spoken in the old language, but not the oldest.

> *Ave Maria, gratia plena, Dominus tecum.*
> *Benedicta tu in mulieribus,*
> *et benedictus fructus ventris tui, Iesus.*
> *Sancta Maria, Mater Dei,*
> *ora pro nobis peccatoribus,*
> *nunc et in hora mortis nostrae. Amen.*

We can't imagine that anyone who lives in the shadow of Christian culture doesn't know this old prayer, so we speak it together, remembering. And then we alter it to suit the sojourn we stand in, the search for a way to connect with the authority and love of the Primal Mother.

Hail, Mary, full of grace. Blessed art thou amongst women and blessed is the fruit of thy Womb. Holy Mary, Mother of all, pray for us now and at the hour of our death.

We look again at the scattering of talismans on the steps, the wounds laid bare, the grief that can't be held alone by any of us. Those talismans are gifts, offerings, tokens of a love so profound that the giver has gone directly to Source, directly to the One who can help and who will help.

In some way, the power structure that stripped away the Goddess from culture after culture, relegating Her to obscurity, to demon, to whore, also maintained this revenant of the Old Ones, this being clad in the color of the sea, whose name is a cognate with the word for the ocean—*mare*. She stands with the crescent Moon at Her feet. A snake curls there, too. These symbols of renewal and transformation are obscured as our attention is drawn to Her crown and the baby in Her arms.

Theotokos. Theatokos. Thea. God-bearer. Goddess-bearer. Goddess.

In this place, among the petals and teddy bears, we remember. We remember a being so powerful, so loving, so relentless in Her support of humanity that She could not be repressed, nor subdued for long. *Thea Aniketos.* Goddess Unconquered.

We look again at the blue and golden image, and She seems to look back at us, Her mouth slightly curved. She has revealed a secret self to us, and we are grateful for sharing a secret with Her. Something about the little smile and the revelation reminds us of another rhyme. *Mary, Mary, quite contrary, how does your garden grow?*

We laugh then and move the teddy to the center of the top step, arranging some of the scattered flowers around its round feet. We like this new Mary we have met, and with the thoughts of cockle shells—the badges of pilgrims past—we go out to admire Her growing garden before turning away from the old basilica and back to our journey.

Thea Aniketos. Adamantaea. Unconquered. Unconquerable.

We move from this strangely comfortable place and rejoin the pilgrims' road far from this mountain town—we next find ourselves in the steppes.

Perceptions

One Goddess who has survived, much diminished, into modern times isn't even considered a Goddess by the majority of people who honor Her. The Blessed Virgin Mary is beloved, but She isn't of quite the same caliber as the triple-aspected male deity with whom She interacts. She is also part of our search for a feral church—a place where She is returned to Her ancient divine status.

The Beatles sang about Her. The Nativity story couldn't be told without Her. And yet this gentle mother called Mary seems always upstaged and downgraded within the lore of Christianity. She is the dutiful wife, the long-suffering mother, and is one of the women who remained throughout Her child's suffering and death, not knowing it was a trick, that Her suffering at his loss would be turned around in a couple of days. Had he whispered the truth to Her? Don't worry, Mama, it's not real?

That isn't part of Her story. She endures. She is described so often as *mater dolorosa*, the sorrowful mother, our Lady of Sorrows. She endures, She remembers all things and ponders them in Her heart. She is "virgin," which is thought by some to mean She never had sex before being impregnated by the spirit of the Abrahamic god. But others have posited that "virgin" may also mean a woman in charge of Her own life and finances.

She has revealed Herself to us as She was and is—a once and future Queen who stands between the world of matter and of spirit. One who is seen all over the world, a traveler as we are. Unconquered and unconquerable. We light your candles and speak your Divine Name—*Theatokos. Thea Aniketos. Adamantaea.*

Chapter 3
LIFE UNDER ICE: CREATING OUR MYTHIC STORY

From the sweet darkness of an old Catholic church, we move now to an unfamiliar place, and the setting is folkloric, a living culture that turns into a place of legend and magic. We leave the familiar and step into a strange world. The Arctic tundra—whether Siberia, Canada, or Alaska—is a place of blinding beauty, of challenge, of danger. The humans who have learned to live with the inhospitable environment are adept at interacting with the spirits of the place, from the foxes and reindeer to the lights of the aurora *aksarnirq*, the sacred ball players who guide the souls of the departed. There is a strangeness in this place, peopled with the grandmothers, the children, the horses, and the dead.

The Journey

Not many visit this place by choice. But people have lived in this cold place since history was recorded, and they traversed it long before that. Those people have traditionally been nomadic, but that is a hard way to follow in the modern world of nations and armies, of mineral extraction and agriculture. Some of the old ways survive in spite of all, and we have spent days now at a gathering of horse people who have come together for horse trading and riding competitions before they head to their winter camping grounds.

Winter is here, as far as we can tell. But we are not as accustomed to the weather on the steppes as our hosts are. They laugh at us as we crack the ice on water buckets and shiver as we wash our faces. *Soft,* they laugh. *You best come with us! Too cold for you!* But we notice them watching the morning sky and nodding to each other. They know it is time to move. Goats, sheep, and horses are milked and cheese is being made. The grazing animals are filling themselves with the rich grasses, already bitten by the night cold.

Most of us are no good at milking but a few are, and they are petted by our hosts, given little treats to encourage them. They are also instructed to teach the rest of us, and by the end of our time, here we are pretty good at milking each of the animals. We even make acceptable cheese. Our hosts laugh and are wild in their exaggerated praise.

On our last night with them, there is a tender and beautiful dinner. It is not only for us—it is the traditional ending ritual before the group moves on. There is feasting, of course—goat is boiled and fragrant with spices. There are ceremonial goodbyes to the land in the same way you would say goodbye to your beloved parents before going away for an extended time. There is crying and laughing, and we are honored to be seated beside our hosts, who drink to our courage and to the success of our vision-work. They have made no secret of their belief that we are crazy and they will find our gnawed bones and hanks of our hair when they return in the spring, but they're resigned to it.

One old woman—who taught us how to make soft cheese from mare's milk—has promised she will collect all our hair and braid it into a rope for the horses. She says it will be very beautiful and we will be proud to be the decoration on such good horses. She laughs a big, broken cackle—the kind you would expect from a very old and very toothless grandmother—and we laugh with her and acknowledge the honor of such a decoration braided by such skilled and ancient hands. Everyone laughs then—we honor them by understanding their teasing way. But we also feel the confusion underneath their teasing. Why would we stay here longer in this place of ice and coming snow? We have tried to explain that it is a journey for us to find our souls, a concept they understand. But they don't know why we can't do that at home in our warm houses, in our own beds. They are puzzled but kind, and their hospitality has meant the world to us.

We are not completely stupid, at least we hope we aren't. In two weeks' time, we have arranged for transport to pick us up and return us to the next place on this pilgrimage. We are being left with adequate shelter and food, probably everything we need. Probably. But if we end here, we know our hair at least will live on, tied onto the halters of the horses.

The next morning dawns too early, and we squat around a small fire with our friends, drinking a yogurt drink and watching the final preparations for their departure. The elders leave much of the work to the younger ones, and then they tell us a few more stories of years past, when the world was better but life was just as hard. They reach down to stroke the broken grass and gesture to the east, reminding us of the road we will travel today.

It isn't an actual road. It isn't even a path. We are carrying a compass and have been told the direction. We are warned to make an offering to the land and to the spirits of each place we stop. They leave us to create the important ceremony that is necessary for our arrival at the place we've been directed to. That is personal, they explain, and we must follow what the spirits tell us to do. We nod and secretly hope we can hear those voices, the ones we have longed to hear.

In no time at all, the group is ready. Some will travel mounted, leading the horses. Others will be herding the other flocks, and some of them will be mounted while others walk. The big change that has happened in the last decade is that gas-powered vans and trucks carry the heavy tents and housewares. These used to travel on wagons, but the modern world does afford the travelers this comfort. The trucks and vans will go ahead of the herds, and the site will be cleared and the housing raised and ready for the rest of the arrivals. Once the herds are secured and tended, the whole group will offer a ceremony and make grateful offerings for the safe journey and the welcome of the land that is their winter quarters.

We stand to honor their journey, waving to them and blowing kisses—which they find hilarious. They bow in our direction three times and we mimic them, with our hands over our hearts. We run to the little grandmother as she is helped into the seat of one of the vans, and we grab her hands and kiss them. She blushes, embarrassed, and pushes us away, laughing.

There is so much excitement as they move, following the old road they and their ancestors have traveled so many times before. The long train is on its way when a young girl jumps down from the back of a loaded truck and gets down on her knees on the flattened grass. She speaks to the land with great earnestness, grabs up a hunk of moss and kisses the bare place where her moss once lay. The truck has slowed down, waiting for her. She runs to jump up on the tailgate of the truck and waves to us one last time. She points to the moss in her hand and yells something that we don't understand. The truck speeds up then and she grabs the side and turns to speak to her friend.

And just like that, they are gone.

It is our turn now. We are supplied with arctic-grade tents and backpacks to hold all we need. Each of us puts on a heavy pack, and we come to stand in a circle facing each other. It's time. Thinking of our friends, we bow to each other three times, then each reaches down to touch the moss. We kiss our fingers and touch the grass. The last of the yogurt is poured out and we turn our faces to the east, into the risen sun.

Our journey should take us two days in and another two days back out, if we move at a steady pace and don't stop too often. We begin slowly, letting our backs and shoulders adjust to the unaccustomed weight. Three people carry compasses and we let them lead us forward. Occasionally, someone in the back stops, takes a good look at where we've come, and then scurries to catch up.

We read about this place some time ago, and most of what we read assured us it was a legend and not a real place at all. Or that it had existed in ages past and that the people of the region had a kind of cultural memory of something long ago destroyed by time or marauding humans. When we first read about it, the idea fired our imaginations, and that was good enough to send us in search of something that held the same sense of liminality. We were intrigued by a threshold into the watery places of the world and the creatures that inhabit them.

Our research kept bringing us back to the steppes, or perhaps the tundra. One of us knew somebody who knew somebody who had a story to tell us. When we heard that story, a way seemed to open for us, a path was made clear, and connections that had seemed impossible were easily made.

The place we felt so called to wasn't a myth, but it was a protected place that few ever saw and almost none stayed for long. It was not difficult to find, but the people of the land and the spirits of the place itself have kept it such a profound secret that the tales of it have fallen into myth and legend.

We were allowed to know because that same old woman who had taught us to make cheese and laughed about collecting the hair from our battered heads had made the journey to it to ask the spirits herself. She had walked with a sack of hard bread and a flask of yogurt, not sleeping until she arrived. There she made her offering and lay down to sleep. When she woke, there was dried fish and fresh water for her breakfast. She knew she had been heard and she knew the answer to her question. Permission was given, predicated on a ceremony and correct offering. She ate the fish, drank some water, and fell asleep again. Her dreams were filled with green water and fishes with the faces of girls. Upon waking, there was a bowl of water-greens to eat and more dried fish. She ate the greens, walked a discreet distance away and peed, then gathered everything up to head home. She bowed three times and left the last bit of sweet bread in thanks for a good outcome. She walked steadily, not often stopping, and the children met her a mile or more from the camp. They held her hands and sang her the song of welcome and brought her a bowl of yogurt, which she drank with gratitude. The rest of the group rose to meet her and she nodded to them, to acknowledge the success of her mission.

Her granddaughter contacted a friend who contacted our friend who contacted us. And so we came to be traveling into the East to meet the Goddesses of this place where moss flows like a river and mares are milked for soft cheese.

The place, in truth and also in legend, is called the Old Water in every language in which it is known. In this windy and arid place, water must be a treasure to be protected. As we walk, we speak of the waters we have known—of the rivers and the waterfalls, the bathtubs, the holy wells. This last one gives us an idea for a ceremony, and we quietly compose it as we walk.

After a couple of brief stops—one for a simple meal—we arrive at a slight indentation in the fields and make ready to rest. The sun is far into the west by now, and we make long shadows on the plains beneath our feet. We set up a circle of tents and light a small and careful fire in the center of them, mainly for company as we are not cooking any food. Our years of reading and watching movies help us to decide to set a watch, and each of us will take a turn sitting at the fire and watching the world around us. Only two hours each, so that no one is sleep-deprived on our trek tomorrow. We will do it in pairs, we decide. And with that, we have a good meal and go to bed, there to dream of water and wind and a young girl and old woman who walk hand-in-hand to sit by the campfire.

It was a blissfully uneventful night. We rise early and remarkably refreshed, breaking our fast and then breaking camp. We head once more into the east but turning slightly northward today, for those are our directions. We are a little slower today and we are talking again as we walk, sharing our dreams and impressions of the days that preceded these. We make a few more stops than we did the day before—it is not that we are particularly tired, but the enormity of what we are doing seems to suddenly be brought home to us. Until now, it has almost been a spiritual vacation where we meet new people and learn something of their lives and their folkways.

But now the full import of why we have come and what we hope to gain from the journey—the pilgrimage—seems heavy on us. Our conversations are more sporadic as though our thoughts have overwhelmed us. We wonder—not for the first or the last time—if we are equal to this task of returning to our wild nature, of finding this feral church.

The birds overhead are the first sign that we are nearing our destination. We see them in the not-so-distant sky, some circling like carrion-feeders or hunters, others darting about. There seems to be a darker blot on the horizon and the westering sun shines a shaft of brightness into the place, like an old-fashioned Hollywood spotlight. We leave our melancholy and apprehension behind us and our pace picks up.

It looks like we imagine a desert oasis might look, though there are no palm trees. But there are shrubs so thick that we can't see what they hide. Because the wind here is never ceasing, these shrubs are low and scrubby. But they are growing around the edges of a small pond, so their foliage must be lush in the summer months. Since we are heading into winter, the leaves are orange and scarlet, made brighter by the last of the sun.

We let our packs fall from our shoulders and approach this shockingly bright place. Here is where the birds come to drink and the raptors to hunt. The hedge is broken in several places, but we stand still, unwilling to move through those gaps just yet.

Someone laughs nervously. This place feels distinctly "otherworldly" and lives up to its reputation as a place between here and there, a liminal place, a portal. We set up our camp as we did the night before. But not in a circle this time. We make a crescent whose open side faces the hedge and the Old Water. We wonder if a fire is permitted but hold off on that until after we have made our offering and ceremony.

We assemble in front of one of the gaps in the hedge. We remove our shoes and our hats, even though the wind is cold here, colder than it had been last night. From our packs and our pockets we bring forth the offerings we have brought with us—there are colorful candies, bits of colored lambs' wool, a shell button from someone's grandmother, a cloutie left over from Brigid's Day. We hold these talismans in our hands and approach the gap in the hedge. We bow three times—we are getting good at remembering this—and then we ornament the gap in the same way as we would "dress" a holy well. All the trinkets are woven into the bright branches, and we cut bits of our hair and add that in, too. After a while, the entryway is marked in beauty and love, and we leave small offerings of food nearer the water itself.

We wait. We try to discern if the ceremony has been completed and the offering accepted. Then we hear—whether it is a trick of the wind and the shrubs—an audible sigh, and the birds, who were silent and suspicious before, sing brightly. We bow three times and slowly return to our camp, to eat our own meal and dream the dreams we may be given. There is no need to set a lookout tonight. We are here, and for now, at least, all is well.

We sleep fitfully, wakened too often by sharp and unfamiliar sounds, disturbed by dreams that make no sense but seem to have much meaning. We huddle in the center of the crescent made by our tents and face the decorated portal that will lead us into the Old Water. In the night, other hands have threaded bright leaves and bits of pond-greens into our well dressing, and the whole of it glows in the morning sun. In the space underneath the arch, there is a careful arrangement of dried fish and leaves made into bowl shapes that hold berries and fresh birds' eggs. We walk slowly to the arch and bow, of course. Then someone softly sings a child's song about a garden walk with coral bells and lilies-of-the-valley on either side. Those of us who know it join in. The sweet song lightens our hearts and, as the sun rises, we finally approach the Old Water.

Last night, the edges of the pond were white with rime ice, solid as the cubes that chill our drinks back home. The plants around the pond have drooped their heads onto the surface of the water, stuck there in those awkward poses. The fish that inhabit this damp place have traveled to the deepest point of the water, and there they drift among the fingered branches of lost trees, almost sleeping, almost still. None disturb them in the chill of the season. No lure is dropped, no kingfisher dives.

This metaphor has burdened too many of us for far too long. We are weighed down by habit, by culture, by family and personal history, and by lives touched by trauma. The ice ceiling is a cunning container: we can look out to see the clouds, the sky, the birds skimming the implacable surface, impatient for the soft water's return.

Listen now to the clicking of fingers tapping ice, fingernails scraping grooves of frost, palms slapping, fists punching. The sounds are rhythmic, lulling us past our discomfort and confusion. We have come to this place with no instructions and no intuition. Some of us are turning away when we hear a splash and realize one of us has fallen in. Like students at a frat party, we shrug our shoulders, hardly bracing ourselves or thinking, and follow suit.

It takes us no time at all to understand that the ice has swiftly firmed itself over us and the edges of the pond are closed up tight. No way out. Our puny strength is no match for the full weight of winter. The ice ceiling—place of cold weight, of guilt, of shame, of unrelenting trauma and memories—will not yield in this resting season. The way out is down, is below, is to continue under. This is slow life. Down in the depths of this place, a place of selkies, of merfolk, and of pregnant seeds.

Down in the depths of this place of rotting leaf and dreaming pond life—here is where we must go to feel free again. Kicking our feet, pushing them against the frozen roof, we turn away from the false, treacherous light and we dive.

Ancient gills from our primordial lives split along our necks, and the cold rush invigorates us as we dive. We will rest in the slimy embrace of Those Who Dwell Beneath, and there we will see what the decomposition of life has to teach us about transformation and mess. We have come to learn how to let go.

The water's temperature seems to rise a bit as we sink lower and lower. There is little left of the surface's filtered light, and we make our way through the pond scum and autumn's split branches. Later, we will discover scratches and oddly shaped bruises, but now we feel the metallic twist of fear in our guts.

We stretch our hands above our heads, anticipating the floor that has turned into another ceiling. Unlike the shield of pond ice we've left behind, the floor is neither smooth nor cold. Our fingers will never find smoothness here and will never touch bottom.

At last we arrive at that dense layer, our fingers grasping the unknowable. Sightless, we feel our way to a place where our knees can settle. The trip down was scary even as our curiosity was tickled. We will do the wisest of things and make the best choices here on the bottom of the pond.

We will rest and be still. We will use our civilization-dulled senses, beginning quietly, feeling our way down on thighs already streaked with leaf mold and rot. Our hands rest on our knees and we send out small pulses of our personal life force. It is intuitive, this sending, as we open channels of wordless communication, like sonar in the cold pond.

The pulses increase in frequency and our bodies relax. There is no time to wonder at the transformation we have undergone or to fear this place that is unknown except in our oldest form. The stillness lasts until we are as at home in this strangeness as we will ever be. The water has cleared around us and we see the dozing fishes who are unconcerned with our presence. Turtles have buried themselves in the ooze, hibernating until their old inner clocks push them to the surface and into the world above. We watch the debris-covered lumps that mark their winter beds, with here and there an occasional bubble rising up.

This weird place is relaxing and comforting after our encounters above. We are merely observing, learning how these other beings survive the winter, resting out of sight. Do they dream as we do? Does the season that has ended replay as they rest, bringing them wisdom to survive the coming season? We think it must be peaceful for them, too, with no predators to torment them, no need to search for food, no reason to find a mate and to raise the next generation of their people. We can see each other quite clearly and sometimes nod to signal that we are okay.

The clear water is suddenly clouded in a thick wave and our vision is obscured. There is movement within the cloud and we are chilled. The water no longer feels safe, we are no longer comfortable. Out of the murky cloud, two fishes swim smoothly in front of us and peer in our direction. They are long and somewhat slim with very long side fins and broad tails. They move back and forth before us, then quickly swim away in the direction they came. The cloud of detritus begins to settle and we do, too. How strange. What were they looking for? Were we a diversion for them as they moved through their water-home? Were they as surprised by us as we were by them?

What we didn't know, what we couldn't have known, is that those fishes were messengers and scouts for the other beings who make their home in the ponds and lakes of the world. The whirling undertow flows toward us again, and this time we are curious and excited. We aren't far into this quest, this pilgrimage or whatever it is. We haven't learned yet to be either fierce or afraid. That will come later, if we are lucky.

No long fishes this time but a sight even more astounding. Three of them this time and they look like mermaids from some dystopian nightmare. They appear neither female nor male, being of the same size and with faces remarkably fishlike. The hair on their narrow heads is heavily textured, like the floating weeds we encountered on the way to this quiet place. Their lower bodies are strong, finned and scaled, and end with a broad caudal fin. The fins at the sides of their bodies look somewhat like human arms but much shorter, and the ends of those fin-arms are quite beautiful, like the fluttering tails of beta fish. Large eyes protrude from the sides of those narrow heads, unblinking goldfish eyes, bulbous and rolling in all directions, the better to keep track of all the little fishes and fishlike creatures that swim all around them.

Their coloration is beautiful and that holds our attention. They are gesturing wildly in our direction, and the little fish swim to us, surrounding us as they circle faster and faster. It is a strange dance, and we realize there is less threat than we thought at first. But the agitation has disrupted the peaceful place, and we no longer feel as though we can stay much longer.

The frantic dancing stops as quickly as it started as fish and fishfolk swim swiftly away, still gesturing, still agitated. We wait until the water has cleared once more and nod to each other. With a jerk of our thumbs, we rise to begin our ascent to the surface. It is then that a silent creature, different from any we have seen, moves toward us on the floor of the pond. It is more humanlike than the others but not really human. The coloring is as bright as the others, but the features are less stark, less strange. It walks on short legs but legs with a broad fringe of fin on the sides and back. The arms are likewise short and finned, and the face is broad with eyes large but facing forward. The creature is a beautiful combination of fish and human, and we know we are looking at our distant kin, descendants of the same ancestors. We chose the land, with excursions into the water, and they chose the water, with excursions onto the land. Both sets of beings can walk—or swim—between these two worlds and still be most at home in one or the other.

The beautiful water-being comes to stand in front of us, and we almost cry to see it bow three times. Maybe we have found a universal gesture of introduction and of welcome. Of course, we bow in return and the water-being claps its finny hands together in surprise. Over one arm there is a basket made from pond-weed and the plants that droop over the surface of the Old Water, and it is held out to us. We move closer and see that it holds the same rich green moss that lives in the world above, the moss the girl took with her to their winter quarters.

Our nomadic friends taught us well. One by one, we take a tiny mound of moss, raise it to our lips, and kiss it. The water-being nods its approval as each piece is kissed and returned. From under the layer of mosses comes a leaf-wrapped package that is presented to us. We take the gift and bow our thanks. We are so tired now from the surprises and the frights, and we, who are more suited to the dry land above, feel the need to go home.

The water-being watches us go with an approving cast to its face. We turn back as we near the cold surface and it has turned, disappearing into the depths of the old pond. The weak sun has nevertheless cracked the ice on the surface, and we stagger out onto the bank, onto the land. We squat there, looking over the water, wondering what we have seen and done. There is a smell of smoke on the air, and we turn to find a cheerful fire burning in a circle of stone in front of our tents.

We walk to it gratefully, rubbing our bodies with our blankets so the friction warms us as we dry off. When we are dressed again and no longer shivering, we sit around our little fire and open the package that was given us in the deep.

It is dried fish and pondweed, a perfect supper.

We sleep fitfully and our dreams are filled with the greenish light of the underwater world. Our companions are migrating whales, galloping horses, and seal-women with their sleek coats. Oysters bring us necklaces of pearls and fish bones. Water fills our lungs and we can fully breathe at last.

Perceptions

Our journey will take us many places, and we are going to meet beings that are familiar, some that seem familiar but aren't, and others that are surprising and unknown. We may find that it is the latter category that feels the most like our interior selves, our true selves. We are traveling out to go in and are getting away from the comfortable and the familiar so that we can peel back the acculturated layers from our communities and families and see what's really underneath that. We tend to go through life being averse to pain and fear—for very good reasons. Some of us have experienced too much of that already, and when those experiences happen in childhood and young adulthood, the damage is long-lasting and deep. It is only natural that the things that bring up those old experiences can throw us right back to that terrified little person who had no one to help them, to stop the trauma.

This journey—this pilgrimage—is not only to seek a connection with our Primal Mothers. It is also where we look those traumas and terrors in the eye. Then we reach in our pockets for our grown-up sense of discernment, of understanding. Is there real danger here, or is it merely the echo of a memory that struck at our souls so hard it left an imprint? Consider. Take your time. Feel your way through it. Then use your good sense, your intelligence, and your hard-won experience to see how you move on from it.

Sometimes we can't move on, not without help. There is help in the form of counselors and therapists. Sometimes a heart-sister or other close friend can act as your sounding board. (Don't forget that you can also be a sounding board for those who love and trust you.) Give yourself the gift of time and of loving yourself enough to work through and move beyond. There will certainly be memories you can't erase. That's how memory works. But giving yourself the time to work through residual guilt or shame can help you drop some of the weight of it, the burden of it. You are worth doing that work, and your pilgrimage to find the feral church will be easier for your lightness of being.

Chapter 4
THE GRASSLANDS AND THE WOMB

In this chapter we travel not only to a new place but to another time. In the high prairie of North America, we have come to set ourselves into a womb of the earth, a place of rest and of challenged fears. We are here together and share this link in the pilgrimage chain.

THE JOURNEY

We blink our eyes against the relentless wind. Those of us with glasses fare a bit better, but we can all feel our skin drying as the wind sucks away any residual moisture. We are standing on a low rise—too small to call a hill—and there is no way we can turn to avoid the wind. There are blessings and beauties here, though. From our vantage point, we can see far in all directions. The sunlight is surprisingly soft, and the colors of the prairie are muted. As far as we can see, there are waving grasses and strange blooms. Acres and acres of this flowing, moving landscape are captivating and strangely soothing.

It seems an odd place to consider our need for healing and our desire for justice. But we have been called to this place for these particular intentions, and so we have come here. It often feels that patience is a significant part of the journey we've chosen, and it is good to learn this early on in our quest. We are collecting beads of wisdom and will string them together when we can. The bead we are offered here may have to be offered again for us to absorb it thoroughly. It's a complex thing we are undertaking, this road to rewilding, uncivilizing, and returning to our deepest source. Perhaps the first part of patience that we are called to learn is patience with ourselves and with the process we have chosen and continue to alter.

This grassland, this prairie world, stretches as far as we can see, and that is pretty far. There was a time in the long history of the land when these fertile places stretched on for millions of acres and were a habitat for an extraordinary number of animals and plants. We have come early in the day to feel ourselves under this vast sky and to understand our small place in this large landscape.

Insects are plentiful here, and because they are, the animals that feed on insects are also plentiful. The insects are thriving because the vast grasslands give them plenty of food and shelter for breeding. The birds and small mammals are abundant because they have plenty to eat, and the larger animals and reptiles do well because they have all those delicious insects. There are prairies dogs, burrowing owls, badgers, and moles here, living both below ground and on the surface.

We have come to encounter all these beings—as well as this sacred land itself—to seek our own way into the profound darkness we all carry, and we have come to pay our respects to the torn history of these places. We will journey into the badgers' burrow before midday to see what we can see.

For now we are quite satisfied with the feel of the place. We walk in a circle to mash down the grass enough to sit on it. Our seat is so cushioned that we feel immediately comfortable and turn to face outward to peer into the tall grass. Each of us has a different view of the extraordinary life in the prairie. One sees a brown bird sitting on her nest and making a staccato peep to warn us away. Another sees a spider with her web close to the ground, tacked between some wild bergamot and something that looks like an artemisia. We reach forward very carefully and squeeze a leaf of each, sniffing our fingers to confirm our guess. The spider seems unconcerned with us and continues her weaving. For the most part, we simply see more grass, grass with thick and well-rooted stems and thin wiry stalks. There are some old seed-heads that survived the stark winds of winter on the plains, and they bend their heads toward us as though they want us to remove the last of their heavy burden so that they can begin the process again.

We are very small compared to the vast acres of grass, even in our little circle. The grass towers over us, providing cover from any approaching predator. We all turn inward and find ourselves gazing at our comrades. We are aware of the plants and animals that surround us, and for the first time here, there is an uneasy feeling that we are not part of this biome. We are the interlopers, we are the intruders.

This uneasy feeling is one we will feel over and over until we grasp one of the profound reasons for this sojourn. If we are to be truly connected to the natural world—a connection we acknowledge but don't often feel—it is vital that we find the courage to open to the wildness of it. We also have to have the good sense to understand when something out there is truly dangerous or when it is merely a reflection of the fear and trauma we carry with us all the time.

Here, in this place, we are going to learn about dealing with our personal histories, as we engage our trauma and spend time in the shadowed world under this grassland. We rise from our nest and move slowly toward an outcropping of rocks not far away. We have been told we will find a badger den there, an uninhabited one, for which we are grateful. Badgers are tricky to encounter at the best of times. We don't want to be caught trespassing in a den. The badger here was between matings and raising her young and was killed not long ago when she was trapped by a wildfire too far from her den to go into it for safety. The place is far too valuable as prairie real estate, and so we have come here now while we can still do our work in the underground part of this world.

Underground. Buried in the soil of Mother Earth. That's our destination. We are returning to a place where healing is possible, where the darkness allows gestation, and where delicious rest invites healing. Here, in this place, in the Womb of the Grasslands.

The sacred womb is a big, smooth hole between two large rocks, and it still smells strongly of badger. We assume it is badger because it smells musky and rank. We stand in this holy healing place and feel a little sick. Surely the badger is not long dead if it smells so strong here? And then the real concern—does it smell so strong here because a badger has come to claim this very fine burrow?

Badgers are not large, about the size of a medium dog, but they are wonderful tunnel diggers and den crafters, with long claws on their front paws and strong forelegs. They have a fiercesome reputation but we have it on good authority that this sett is really empty, so we proceed. We are already getting used to the skunkish smell. Now it is the narrow opening and the impending darkness we are considering. A few of us have those handy headlamps and that should help, but the point of being underground is to experience the dark. We agree that we will use them to light our way through the tunnel and into the den. Two of us decide the sensible thing to do is to send those with headlamps in to see how far the den is and if it will fit us all. Relieved to have a wait, we watch as they wiggle through the smooth mouth and see the feet of the second one disappear.

We share some water as we wait and watch the sun's movement into midafternoon. It seems an age, but at last we hear voices echoing through the tunnel—and some laughter—and there they are! Dirty but fine.

As it turns out, the den is about a ten-minute crawl in, and the tunnel widens almost as soon as feet disappear inside it. It is more crawling than wiggling, and we hear that report with some relief. The air is good, if a little close. There are tunnels that branch off the main one, and we conclude that some of those must be to allow fresh air in.

The den is quite large—in the middle it is tall enough to sit up, but most of us will need to recline. That is fine. We are looking for a birth and womb experience and reclining was how we all assumed that would happen. We are mildly concerned about the extra tunnels, but our intrepid explorers assure us they are much smaller and seem less used than the main way in—we are unlikely to get lost. Perhaps most importantly, there is no sign of a resident badger.

We circle up and hold hands, looking carefully at each other. We are all a little scared, if we are honest. But we are also determined. There is so much pain in some of these eyes, and we all feel there are answers in this exercise in the belly of the prairie.

One by one, we wiggle into the entrance. We have put the most uneasy in the center of the group where they can be touched and encouraged by steady hands. The scouts were right—the going isn't bad on hands and knees. The floor is smooth and there are remains of soft grass that were no doubt brought in to soften the nest for a birthing badger as well as her cubs. We go slowly and are quiet except for our breathing and the occasional swear about knees and elbows. Several smaller openings indicate the ventilation tunnels, and we imagine we can feel a slight breeze as we crawl by.

We reach the den more quickly than we thought, and it is indeed large enough for all of us. We stretch out along the walls and a couple of us with headlamps sit in the middle, chandelier-like. The few other headlamps are turned off and we allow ourselves a few minutes of settling in before we give ourselves over to the darkness. We breathe deeply in spite of the badger musk. The dried grasses still give off their sweet scent.

At last, we are all ready. As the last lights are turned off, we imagine how a mama badger would look if she came home to find all these prone humans. There was giggling as the den was plunged into its customary darkness.

Some grumbling at first. This one can't get comfortable, that one sneezes several times with a sound that echoes around the den. A soft voice says, *Do badgers sneeze?* and there is a soft giggle again. Then we are all silent.

To be comfortably underground, stretched out on a bed of soft grasses, breathing fairly fresh air is not the same as being buried alive. Let's be very clear about that. There is always a risk of claustrophobia, of course, and a primal fear of the earth caving in on top of us. But the risk we face in the darkness here is not that risk. We are alone with our personal histories. We lie in the darkness with our demons and our traumas. There is a kind of death here. But it is the death that leads to rebirth, to healing, to freedom from the heavy baggage we have all carried for far too long.

Too many of us walk through the world like Dickens's Jacob Marley. We carry the weight of our own lives as well as what living those lives accumulates—the barnacles of regret and pain, of abuse and shame. Bound in the double helix of our DNA, we may also carry the collective histories of our genetic ancestors and the ache of their longing for the basic necessities of life. In addition to these heavy chains, those of us who are good listeners (the baristas and booksellers of the world) often pick up the baggage of all the people who came to ease their burdens, either by hearing them relate their misfortunes or by actively taking part in the solutions. We may also hold revenants of daily news briefs, of social media's peculiar kinships, of the state of the planet and of the parts of it with which we dwell.

We all lie in the darkness sometimes, whether literally (as we are now) or metaphorically. A night of poor sleeping and dramatic dreams often sets us up for the seemingly endless recycling of what has been done, what hasn't been done, what is left to be done, ad nauseam. The sunrise sees us more tired and fraught than when we went to bed. Then the daylight cycle begins of too much to be done in too little time, or suppressing any joy until the "work" is done. Then we go back to bed too wired for restful sleep, and the darkness becomes a prison of our thoughts, our inadequacies, our hopes dissolving into anxious stasis.

As we lie here, we are alone, each in our contained bubble of darkness, of quiet, for now all of us are still and breathing so shallowly that no sound can be heard, not even the tumble of a little soil from the dug-out walls. We wait. We breathe. Our eyes adjust somewhat to the darkness, and we realize it is not complete. There is a deep grayness here that doesn't give us enough light to make out any details of the tiny world around us, but enough to comfort the ones who really hate to be shut in. For the most part, though, we are lying here with our eyelids closed. Lying with all of Marley's weight on us, trying to make our minds still enough to let our souls speak.

We think of the vast acres of grassland about us, stretching far in all directions. We wonder how many generations of badgers have denned in this sett. We remember the broad sky of the world above and the foretelling clouds that warn us of weather and offer us dreams. One by one, we release some fear—not all—and we allow ourselves the freedom of remembrance.

We are the drifting ones then. From earliest childhood woundings to the harshness we ourselves dealt out to someone only last week, we tally through the credit and debit sheets of our lives. Here the bullying in school, the bullying at home. There the violent encounter that the perpetrator insisted was love. We feel again the loneliness of losing what is familiar, whether human or material, and how we must never allow that emptiness to be seen to affect our work or our relationships. We are wrapped in the grief that goes ungrieved, in the fury that must be sucked up and sucked down to fill us with acrid nothingness.

It is no longer silent in the den. There are muttered words, cries, sniffling, moans of relived pain. We don't know how long we lie there, feeling it, reliving it. But then an odd thing happens and the brightness of the prairie above us begins to seep into those holes of nothingness inside us. At first, only a glimmer, like the glow of a lightning bug. The sounds around us begin to change, and this place in the earth, in the primordial Goddess of us all, is now a womb and a place to commence a radical and profound healing. We feel nourishment from the earth around us and nurturing from the soul of this great Mother who has birthed us and is birthing us again.

There is gasping now, and a sigh, followed by a laugh of pure happiness. The den feels as huge as a ballroom, a place where we can grow as large as we want but still drink in the love and power that flows into the empty bellies we have carried for so long. Someone near the center sits up and whispers, *Do you all feel that?* There are murmurings all around but none are ready to speak yet, to discuss, to dissect. We are drinking it all in, eating it up, filling ourselves as we have never been able to do before.

This prairie womb has given us a dark place in which to relive, then release, over and over. The releasing does not make us feel emptier—instead we are refilling with something useable and valuable, something that can sustain us when we are no longer in this safe and quiet place that we have conjured and has been given to us by our oldest and most loving kindred, the planet herself as Mother, as Birther, as Goddess.

We are stirring now, too restless to stay down for much longer. We are all thinking of the world above, wondering if this feeling will settle into our bones, whether it will stay with us throughout our journey. Murmurings all around and some of us moving from our backs onto our hands and knees, readying for the tunnel into the endless grasslands.

At first we don't notice the sound, but soon there is no mistaking that sudden change in the den and in each of us. We feel it before we hear it, though in our excitement we may have thought the pounding was our hearts coming back to life. We flatten ourselves to the walls and the floor and the earth itself begins to move. The old fears fly back into us. Is it an earthquake? A cave-in? Both seem improbable in this old and much-used place. We breathe and feel a little better. Now the sound and the movement are intertwined. Both grow in intensity until they are directly over us. We cover our faces with our hands because this den, in spite of its age, shakes loose soil from above us and beside us.

The sound continues moving over us and away from us. It seems to us that it goes on for hours, though it is only a few moments because it is a small herd, not an endless stream of bison galloping across the great fields. The sound lessens, as does the shaking, and we begin our climb out of the womb that is spitting us out now. The first of us hangs back until there is only a distant rumble and retreating sound. Then one by one, we are reborn into a world of dust, with the smell of crushed plants and shaggy beasts in our nostrils.

Whether we are considering birth as a literal transition or a metaphorical one, it is a life-altering event. Our birth here, from the smelly sett womb of this Mother World, begins a new way of seeing and a new way of knowing what it is we see. We will go forward on unsteady toddler legs, but soon we will walk with confidence, then run. And then we shall fly.

We stand at last and watch the dark mass still moving away from us. Our shoulders and backs are stiff and achy and there is much stretching and grunting. The sun is much lower in the sky than before, and soon it will be twilight on the grasslands. We dust ourselves off and turn back to see the wide swathe that the bison trampled on their way to their next grazing land. Did they gallop with joy, feeling the grass on their bellies and noses? Do they grow exultant in their pounding hooves connecting with the solid ground beneath them? Are they aware of the beauty of this land that supplies everything they want or need, and do they love their prairie home?

Of course, we whisper. *Of course.*

Perceptions

Many books and conferences and sessions with counselors focus on the modern human need to come to terms with our cultural wounds. We carry not only the personal pains and regrets but also the collective grief and hurt of our ancestors, passed down to us as a warning—and as a road to genuine kinship with the rest of the biosphere. Too often, we have masked this through our addictions, our abuse of our kindred and the natural world, and by passing the trauma on to those with whom we enter relationships.

You know that smell from dead skunks on country roads or too-close encounters with bear and fox. It's the musky smell of life unfettered, of lust for breeding, of continuing the species no matter what. That smell signifies wild nature at its most potent. Look around you at all the birds in springtime, making nests and mating, sending trills of combat-readiness into the morning light. Look at the new puppy who is suddenly not so little and is finding an expression of his drive to breed by humping the couch or your leg. Here is the backstory of birth, the pheromones insistent and the womb waiting. We carry with us the lingering aroma of amniotic fluid, blood, and mothers' milk. We breathe in the heritage of our birthing in every sense of that word. Let us never forget to honor the birthing and the One Who Births. Whether we have chosen literal parenthood or not, our duty is to birth a better place for all the births to come.

Chapter 5
Sand and Monsters

We wander now into the desert, and we are well-stocked and prepared for a dangerous climate that requires our attention to all details and also allows us to indulge in the shock of newness and unfamiliarity. Here be monsters. We be monsters.

The Journey

Under the protection of a soft awning, we are led to places already set for us. There is a table laden with plates of food, and heavy pitchers of cool drinks are encircled with cups awaiting our hands and lips. We fall on the food hungrily, for we have walked far with little respite. Our souls bear the jagged imprints of experience and painful discovery. After a while, when we have slowed our pace, we are offered soaking tubs of water, scattered with the herbs of high summer. The plates of delicacies look barely touched, and each of us takes a few sweetmeats with us as we turn to face the west. Our faces are clean for now and our bellies full.

As do our ancestors in the Summerlands, we wait in this halfway house and pause to consider where we have been.

The sand of the desert floor is the color of jewels—sapphire, ruby, emerald, topaz—and it appears like a rich and sudden carpet on the edge of this safe oasis. Our hands are filled with dates and figs, our mouths perfumed with these ancient, biblical fruits. The waterskins lay across our strong shoulders and across the backs of the pack animals that wait under the cool of the palm trees.

Why would we leave such a place, where water splashes into tiled fountains, where there is plenty, comfort, safety? What drives us to flee from this easy simplicity, to seek out searing light and thirst? There is no guarantee of survival in this fierce land. But we have learned from our mothers and our grandmothers that there is no guarantee of survival anywhere, anytime. Only we can save ourselves—no one will hear our call or heed our cries or come to rescue us even if they hear the anguish from our dry, blistered lips.

We are set on a journey our hearts demand, to meet the vicious spirits of this place. Our journey is one of longing and revelation. We move across this shattered carpet of jeweled sand to encounter the monsters that are rumored to live in the wild. What is not known is the fierce temptation—as we learn about the abiding harshness of this world—to deny the sweetness in order to test ourselves to the limit. Monsters ourselves—

unnatural and broken—we go in search of these thorny and spiked Goddess-monsters, these hags, these horrors. The petals of our flower crowns, shriveled, parched, fall down our breasts to the dry sand.

In our pockets, we carry three things—a crust of bread, a very sharp knife, and a packet of seed. These are charms for luck, talismans for traveling mercies. It is madness to carry so little into such a dreadful place. But we are mad. The overculture and our collective histories have driven us to the very edge of madness. We are eldritch creatures—strays who have wandered away, strayed from the approved paths. Straying still into the wild, onto the path taken by those brave ancestor-girls who meet a wise woman disguised as a witch and a witch disguised as a wise woman, for they are exactly the same thing.

We make sure our animals have a last drink of water and that our packs are secured, and we set off. One of us laments the loss of the brightly colored sand, for the way ahead is a monotone of cream and pale gold. We dare not stop to drink, though the breeze is making us thirsty. We have only the supplies we bring with us and have no idea how long this part will take.

We are beginning to slow our step as the wind suddenly drops. This is what we were expecting. This is what we dreaded. We are careful to shield our heads and faces with our clothing as we move steadily toward those hills. Steadily, carefully. The people in the front shout a warning about a desert viper winding its way toward our group. We stop then and wait, and it continues on its way in its own dance across the desert, not troubling us at all, attending to its own business as we are to ours.

But where did it come from, that fat snake? Does it live under the desert floor and pop up only to travel to the next den? None of us knows the answer. None have studied the desert or the creatures that thrive in such a place. Now we are on guard.

The desert wind is surprisingly cool, a breeze that dries the sweat on our faces. The sun is barely over the tops of the low hills, and that is our destination, the meeting point for this part of our schooling. We are moving faster than we probably should, but we hope to take advantage of the coolness to get as far as we can before the sun is too high, wondering what we will encounter next. Will it be unconcerned, or threatened?

The added anxiety is not a blessing. Since we have already come to a stop, we unpack water from our bags and sip it, as we have been advised. Not gulping. It gives us time to fret and worry, and we must refocus our attention on those hills.

We begin again, without the blessing of the breeze. There is wind somewhere, though, because we see a little dust devil between us and our destination. Curious. It is moving fast and we seem to be walking to meet it. As things do in the desert, it appears to whirl faster as it moves directly toward us. Perhaps we are remembering the cooling breeze. Perhaps we are tired and focused on the hills. Whatever the reason, this now-towering whirl of dust is bearing down on us with some speed, and we have stopped in our tracks, covering our mouths and noses and moving closer together.

It twists itself into three separate columns of dust and smoke. We are surrounded by them and couldn't run if we wanted to. The dust thins now, flying away bit by bit to reveal a fantastic vision, three fantastic visions.

One is a being with a woman's body and the head of a bird. Another is a dragon-like creature with the head of a woman, and the third, though we are not quite sure, is a jinn. That one at least makes sense since we are in the desert. But the other two are creatures from stone stelae, from museum exhibits on the Middle East. They traveled with the old nomads in this region, wanderers themselves, seeking encounters with others like themselves, whom they never find. They are the last—or perhaps the only ones—of their kind, and they have begun traveling together in this whirl of smoke and sand. We suspect the snake was their scout and forerunner, and we stand huddled together, more confused than frightened, for there is something sad about them, something lost and grieving. Any fear we felt at the sight of these travelers soon dissipates and our curiosity rises to the fore.

The jinn is the most human looking and that being is the first to address us. The words—if they are words—are like stones dropped on tile, staccato and undefinable. There is a chiming quality to the rhythm and the tone, and it changes to the ringing of small bells. The jinn shakes its head and holds out its hands to calm its companions. It tries again.

This time the words are words, but they are not words we know. Perhaps it is the ancient tongue of the First People—full of clicks and sighs, with many gestures and facial twitches. We aren't sure what our response should be, and the jinn is getting frustrated. We pull the scarves down from our faces and hold out our hands, flat and palms up, toward these odd creatures. The jinn stops speaking. Someone in our little company begins to sing, very softly. We all know the tune and we join in, our hands still stretched out.

The dragon-woman joins us and the bird-woman begins to dance, her curved beak pointing here, then there. The dragon-woman doesn't know the tune so she sings a counter one, harmonizing, her long tail raising dust from the desert's floor. The jinn begins to nod its head, too. What a bizarre moment in time. We have so much to learn in our quest for connection to the Divine, and we are coming to realize that everything is divine, every being is holy. This peculiar concert continues until the jinn stamps its foot and holds up its hands for silence. The gesture feels like a request and not a command, so we all watch the jinn's face for its intention or concerns.

Mimicking our earlier gesture, the jinn now holds out its hands toward us, palms up. The bird-woman does the same. The dragon-woman has no hands, but she nods her head deeply in a kind of bow. We repeat the gesture and bow to the dragon-woman, then the bird-woman, and last, the jinn. There is a broad smile on the dragon's face and the jinn begins to smile, too.

This is good. We remember our pockets and reach in, removing a few of the stored seeds we carry. Stepping forward slowly, we put the seeds into the outstretched hands of the jinn and the bird-woman and they fold their long fingers over their palms. We aren't sure what to do for the dragon-woman and we gather around her, pondering. Several of us remove strands of lapis beads from our necks and hold them up to her. She bends her beautiful head toward us, and we slip the beads over her head and down her slender neck. Then we return to our huddle and wait.

The breeze returns then and the hands that are holding seeds are raised high so that the wind may carry them to fruitful places. It also raises pillars of dust that whip around the three beings, pulling them together and slowly hiding them from our sight. We cover our mouths and noses and begin the song again, muffled but good. We hear the voice of the dragon-woman as she adds the harmony. The tower of swirling dust and smoke is lifted up, up, and up, and as it spins away, we hear the voice of the jinn, speaking the words of the First People, in a kind of benediction.

We knew that this part of our journey would see us in some strange places, learning from some strange beings. But if we have learned nothing else, we understand that if we challenge the Goddess by challenging ourselves, the Divines happily join in to make sure we get the right dosage, the proper frequency, and are filled with all we hunger for. Even when we feel we have finished and received the wisdom we opened ourselves to learning, it is vital to consider that we have consciously yoked ourselves to a wild beast. We are terribly aware that we are not in charge of this journey and are unsure of the ultimate destination. The road will narrow, grow stonier, collapse into a hole, and rise again as a sheer cliff. We will crawl and soar, spot the shadow of the feral church as a mirage along a ridgeline. We will march like little soldiers and run mad like a forest fire pursues us.

We have no time to marvel, for the sun is very high now and our sturdy pack animals will suffer if we don't move on. The hills seem much closer, and we suspect the encounter with those strange spirits may have moved us closer to our goal, without our knowing it. At one time we would have doubted that possibility, but we have seen much in our search and at least we will have a shorter distance to walk than we had before. And a sweet memory of an encounter with spirits that was challenging but ended well.

We move on. The sun is beginning to lower slightly toward the west, and we notice the impossibly long shadows we leave on the golden ground. We are very close indeed when we hear a whistling sound and peer into the hills, squinting in the light. There is a slash of green along the side of one of them, and that is where the sound seems to originate. We drink some water, eat some dates, and pick up the pace then. It could be a mirage, of course, a trick of the light and of our dizzy heads. But it seems to be a promise of something like the comfort we left behind.

Perceptions

The cultures in which most of us abide encourage us to behave in certain societally approved ways. In our bid to separate ourselves from these trappings, we can choose from a number of strategies. We can make ourselves small to avoid notice, which has been a moderately successful option for women and minorities for a long time. Keeping your head down and not rocking the proverbial boat has no guarantees, though. If you are successfully invisible, someone else can draw attention to you (whether deliberately or accidentally). You'll find yourself with no practice in shielding yourself or countering unwanted attention because you've not been confronted with it before and don't have effective experience. You can choose the route that proposes it's easier to get forgiveness than permission and use your best intuition about the situations you encounter—that will help you select from the popular quartet of fly, freeze, fight, and fawn.

Both options serve to stifle your true self. They force you to armor up or to wrap yourself in some sort of cultural invisibility cloak. Both options are successful strategies for dealing with hierarchy, with patriarchy, with the violence inherent in those systems. There is another way. You can choose the danger of rebellion, the certainty of change, and feel the fury, the fear, and the frustration that these other tactics set loose in you. A day of meeting the strangers in the desert or running wild with maenads can set you up for more courage in your daily life and the gumption to work for the change you see as necessary in the world.

Chapter 6
WILD WOMEN, WITCHES, MAENADS

The maenads are characters from Greek antiquity, but they are also an archetype of how women will behave without the pressure to conform that culture imposes. Free people are dangerous people—especially to the status quo. We encounter them now as we arrive at that distant oasis and join their frantic and delicious dance.

THE JOURNEY

We are here and here is the unknown but not the unknowable. Here, so we have come to believe, the maenads shriek and howl like dogs, their way prepared by Fear and her sister Terror, along with their granddam Dread. These ancient maenads roam the barren places, the abandoned places, the forbidden places. At the center of the maelstrom is a spirit who was betrayed by her family and begged to be free to wander the hills, dancing. In the old writing, she was merely known as the sacrificial daughter of the soldier Jephthah.

It is not a mirage. It is a green gorge on the side of the hill, and we approach it with joy. It is a pretty place, but instinctively, we are moving to higher ground, and so we climb beside the glade, heading for the highest point in this range of hills. The sand of the desert floor has become a firm foundation of clay and stone, easy to walk up. The climb is not very long or arduous, for which we are grateful.

We step into a high, clear place that is set with laden olive trees. Some of the trees' bony fingers reach up to the sky and others point downward to the arid soil of this ridge. They stretch and sometimes break, sticks and olives falling to join the dust below. This is the land of maenads, of wild women, of hags. We are not alone in this place any more than we were alone in the vast desert.

Three women are about their work in the clearing amid the olive trees. They have far older names, names that can barely be pronounced by weak modern tongues, but we call the three beings in the olive grove Fear, Terror, and Dread. They often gather here with the spirits of the place and the wild women. Two of them, at first glance, seem young, and the third looks remarkably old, her face a series of gorges and empty riverbeds. The young ones are Fear and Terror. The old woman should never be addressed directly, for to do so assures the speaker of bad luck. Her name translates to Dread, though she will not answer to that.

They do not acknowledge us but go about their tasks. We put down our burdens, carefully moving our pack animals to the dappled shade of the olive trees. We give them grain to eat, and they drink deeply from the fresh spring that also waters the olives.

A fire is being laid by one sister and the other stands at the edge of the olive grove, waiting for the wild folk and maenads who always join the dance. The old granddam is seated on the ground, eyes closed. Fear rubs her plump hands together and a swirl of perfumed smoke twists through her thumbs. She kneels to set the new fire carefully onto the dry leaves and twigs. The fire catches as she sings across it, her shrill waking song invigorating the flame, encouraging it as it roars up, devouring more fuel. Fear straightens up and steps into the smoke and toward the fire. The living dance of firelight is enchanting as we move toward it, following the sister into the smoke.

It is a lovely picture, isn't it? Evocative. You can almost hear the heart-tugging music leading us to relax. In the air, there is a gentle sense of expectation.

Tick. Tick. Tick. Tick.

The smoke from the cheerful fire belches up, growing dense, its pleasant herbal scent changed to tar and iron. Fear raises her arm as a signal, and a crowd of spirit folk creep from the shelter of the stones and approach the fire. Among them, solid in the smoke, are old mothers bent almost double with the weight of heavy, hard staves. These make their way to the old granddam.

The spirit folk begin a stately dance, formal and slow. They look over their shoulders at Fear and Terror, wondering about the course of the evening's events. The bent spirit-mothers surround old Dread, smothering her in interlocking circles, and seat themselves around her, preparing for the council. Her eyelids flutter and she smiles a chilling smile. The smoke from the fire also envelopes her, and it is impossible to tell the spirit-folk from the acrid vapor.

We are not sure of ourselves, not at all. We were more confident with those desert spirits, exploring ways to interact with beings we did not know. These are women and yet they aren't. They aren't like any women we've known. Quite a crowd is gathering near the fire, and we are not sure of our welcome there.

In the midst of this uncertainty, the old woman opens her eyes, milky and unseeing, but she turns her face toward us and nods her head. She gestures toward us and we obey. The eyes of the old women seated around her work perfectly well, and they use them to give us a thorough inspection. Their work complete, they shoo us away with their flapping hands and filthy skirts, and we turn to the dance.

It is no longer a stately thing, and the music has changed. It might be best not to talk of it as music when it is the whirl of pipes and desert winds. There are screams of birth in it and cries of death and dismemberment. The maenads carry their personal history with them, and it crashes through the dance and the stench of the fire.

We watch, unmoving. A trembling seizes our arms, and they shake all around us, as our feet and legs thrust us into the maenad dance. We try to control what our bodies are doing, but our spirits soon join in the violence of the physical movements. The maenads laugh at us and the spirit-folk watch us carefully, as do the old women. Fear and Terror have left the fireside and joined the dance, shaking skin drums with bells, shrieking, crying.

The power in the olive grove is rising with the smoke. With each foot that pounds onto the ground, more ancient energy is released into the dance. We are in frenzy, in that state of desperate need before the release of orgasm, and the frenzy is prolonged into madness. The maenads rip at our hair and rend our faces and still we dance. The rhythm of drum and the shrill of pipes drives us faster and faster and we are leaping across the fire into each other's arms, pushing, scratching, squeezing.

A branch is lifted from the fire and a great cry goes up—*Io! Io!*—and all echo the cry as one maenad leaps through the fire and runs down the hill. We all follow, leaping, laughing, weeping, and calling out—*Burn it all! Burn it down!*

The spirit-folk follow at a careful distance. What happens in the time that follows is blurry to all of us when we talk about it later. Of all the pieces of our sojourn that we will relate in the time to come, this wild hunt with the maenads is never mentioned except in passing. Much was lost in the maelstrom, but much was also cleared away. Our scalding personal histories joined the lore and legend of the maenads that night, and we set down scorched burdens of our own, burdens that had unmade our true selves for such a large part of our lives. We return to the fire with scars achieved and with old scars unmade. Such is the work of the maenads, and when they have welcomed you to the hunt, you will taste how fierce healing can be. Fierce, thorough, redemptive.

Exhausted and bleeding, holding each other up as we can, we leave the maenads and return to the fire, which has burned very low and smells once more of sweet herbs and renewal.

We move to sit with the old women, and they shoo us away to the fire, where the sisters are waiting with cool water and some bread. The pack animals raise their heads curiously, then return unimpressed to their grazing.

At last, we are acceptable to the old women, and we return for their counsel. We sit around blind Dread as she takes up a hank of wool and spins it in her bony fingers. We are glad of the rest and the darkness. Fear tends the fire, and it brightens our circle as we wait for words or gestures to direct us forward.

The hag-women are less patient than we are—or maybe less tired—and they bring the blind woman a cup of water and a clod of honeycomb. Her eyes do not open as she sucks the wax, the honey coating her fingers and running down her chin. The honey depleted, she chews the comb and then spits out the leavings before drinking down the water.

When she speaks, her voice is clear as the night sky above us, a voice as young as she is old. It is a voice full of springtime and snowmelt. Her old face, sticky with honey and grimed with soot, is as fair as wild roses, and she begins to sing.

Her song is full of the lore of women and of the days when Goddesses walked the garden of the world. The young world was filled with music and dancing, with babies being birthed from fertile mothers into a world of promise and beauty. There was plenty in those days, and the people grew wise and good. Some land was tended, other land left free because land was a part of the network of families, the elder kindred, like trees and rivers, like mountains and roving creatures.

But the world and the people grew old and tired. Some came to be resentful of the wild lands and the people and the whole of the world was changed. Goddesses retreated into their sacred places, only to have those places laid bare, ransacked, and spoiled. Now in this time, the old ones were finding their ways back to the people who could hear the voices and the lore.

We understand that this is not history but metaphor, and we understand that we are at the point of another great change. We hear ourselves likened to the raven and the mouse who bring messages to those who can hear them and to the scorpion and the lightning who fly into the world as avengers. These are some of the roles we must bear now, as we return to our pilgrim road. Some among us will serve as messengers and others as avengers.

We sleep under the cold stars and wake alone to an equally cold fire. All the others have returned to wherever they bide, and the entire area is clean and barren. We wash ourselves, prepare the animals, and return to the road.

Perceptions

The trope of the wild and undomesticated human occupies an important place in the world's folklore and history. This being usually appears out of nowhere and may speak a strange language and wear odd clothing. This person is seen as human, not a spirit being, but doesn't behave the way society demands or expects. Seen as a chaotic danger to the order of the state, these outsiders are often driven out of civilization to live out their lives without contaminating what is thought of as the natural order.

Maenads are driven by religious frenzy to flee the domestic word and live in the woods and plains, worshipping Dionysos with the wild abandon of unsanctioned sex, violence, orgies of eating, and drinking intoxicants. They are a safe outlet for the stressors of the state, a safe way to vent potential rebellion and circumvent the fury of abused citizens.

But consider this: the people who live within the confines of modern trauma culture also need a way to release uncontrollable emotions. You need that, I need that. It is up to each of us to find the means and the freedom to access these safety valves for the good of our overall health, mental, physical, emotional.

The spirits on these journeys have more to teach us about the smothering niceties of culture. We have met the wildest of us, at least for now.

Chapter 7
MOTHER NATURE

How appropriate that we often refer to the biosphere as "Mother Nature" or "Mother Earth." Our food comes from her soil, as does our shelter, and everything that sustains human life is bound into the body of the planet. As we are discovering on this pilgrim road, there are places folded into the places we know and beings unseen that inhabit those folds in the strong fabric of time and space. These encounters present us with opportunities to broaden what know and how we proceed.

THE JOURNEY

Of course we feel it—the crumbling of environmental integrity. Daily we hear the terrible news of another species targeted, another vulnerable place breached and destroyed, and another human community given up as lost. It is our souls and our collective soul that are surrendered in the sacrifice zones of the mighty.

Day by day, we absorb the beatings given and marvel at the endurance of the land. The resilience of the life force in the face of this juggernaut of human greed. Not all humans, of course. The peasants remain peasants, scratching a living from poor soil or resentful convenience store customers, sometimes with minimal aid from charity or government.

We go now to the chalk country, chalk now because it was once part of the ancient ocean's floor. We are here to learn some country ceremonies and to walk inside a hollow hill.

We have wandered down a straight dirt road, the shoulders of which are well tended and the ditches weeded and cleared. The chalk hills rise in the near distance, and we glimpse them through breaks in the hedges on either side. The birds and insects ahead of us are bold in their song, and we find such pleasure in a turn of the head. How the sound changes, growing loud as we approach and fading as we walk on. There are autumn leaves falling here, and they remind us that the season is swapping places with the season to come. We shuffle through them, admiring the colors, dreaming of autumn.

The bee yard lies at the edge of the pasture and shares the electric fence that keeps the fat ponies inside their paddock. Those ponies spend their days pulling up clover with their big teeth and chewing thoughtfully as they gaze around them. Sometimes they roll in contentment, too round to roll all the way over, but blissful nonetheless.

Every morning, a trio of stout girls runs to the gate and climbs over it, careful not to touch the charged fence. The ponies shake their clever heads and trot to meet them, whinnying as the girls shout their names. It is a merry meeting, filled with hugs and carroty kisses.

The ponies stand very still as the girls scramble onto their backs and twist their strong fingers into the tossing manes. They head out into the meadow, sometimes at a trot, sometimes at a surprisingly smooth gallop with the girls leaning over the ponies' necks. They end at the little pond opposite the bee yard where the ponies shrug the girls off their backs and bend their mouths to the water. The girls drink, too, cupping the sweet pond water into their mouths. They splash each other and then the ponies, who toss their heads and saunter away.

The girls wander past the bee yard and stand dripping for a moment, watching the coming and going of each hive. They remember there is a queen inside, and they bow solemnly to the mysterious boxes, as they have been taught to do. Then they follow the ponies back to the other side of the pasture, picking red clover flowers for their hair as they go.

The bees pay little notice to this gentle, daily pantomime, for they are always about the business of the hive. The average life of a worker bee is about four weeks, depending on the season, and the work of keeping the hive strong is strenuous and demanding. They gather pollen and nectar for bee bread and for honey, and they feed the larval bees with royal jelly early on before that precious substance is reserved for the ones that will develop into new queens.

The worker bees' short lives are busy as well as fruitful, as they fill the wooden hive boxes with honey for the queen and her enormous and ever-growing family.

It is a warm day so the hives are terribly active, as bees fly swift and true to land on the little strip of wood that is the hive's front porch. There they bump into workers waiting to enter and others that are set to fly. We approach amid a cloud of fliers only aware of us as we get near the boxes.

We stop, as the girls did, a few feet away. The landings and takeoffs are mesmerizing. We notice a different movement on the top of the hive boxes. The forager bee, her saddle bags full of orange pollen, is in the center of a small group of other bees. They seem to be watching her intently as she moves in an observable pattern. Another bee joins the little group and enacts a similar dance.

We move closer, but not as slowly as the hive would like. We are stopped mid-step by bees flying to our faces, warning us off. We wait. Each of us is confronted by such a warrior, and we have enough sense to be quiet and still. This is no gentle dance. The bee buzzes close to the face as a warning to come no further. Back and forth, obviously ready to give her life to protect the hive. The back-and-forth then extends down our bodies and she zigzags quickly, evaluating the danger. Some of us have had harsh encounters with stinging insects, and there is anxiety and no little fear as the scout bees continue their discernment process.

At last, we are cleared. The bees return to their primary work and we move a bit closer, turning our attention again to the dancers. But they are gone. Never mind. We have our own work here and we speak briefly about how we shall proceed.

In the land of the monster women, we were taught so much about venting our fury as we take on the responsibility that only we can bear, and we learned it well. The maenads showed us our own wild and vicious dances and the hag-women brought us into council to explain our role as messengers and avengers. We also learned of an older connection between simple people and the bees they farmed for honey. That is why we are here at last, in this beautiful place.

In olden times, as wives' tales sometimes begin, every garden held a skep of honeybees. They were fat and golden, content in serving their mother and sisters. The resident colonies in the woven skeps were hardly different from the wild bees whose great waxen combs thronged the crevices in the rock face or the limbs of ancient trees. The skeps placed the bees into an easy and direct relationship with the flowers and fruits trees in the garden, and the wild bees had to roam farther afield.

By necessity, the skep colonies were often visited by humans who also dwelt in the gardens and orchards. These humans would choose a different colony every autumn to rob of its honey. Most of the bees' hard-earned honey was removed, as was the queen and many of her children. They were moved to a new, freshly woven skep and the old one was burned. In the spring, it would all begin again. The land was tended and the gardens were not poisoned, as they often are today. Bees were neither livestock nor pets but a separate kingdom that perched at the end of the garden under the orchard.

The special status of these magic creatures was reflected in the way the woman of the house interacted with the hive. These good stewards had learned from their own mothers that—above and beyond the wonderful honey—the bees were a helpful and lucky part of any homestead. The flowers were so bright and the apple trees so laden with fruit because the bees were magnificent pollinators. They were greedy to fill the skeps with pollen and nectar, and this kept them moving from blossom to blossom, doing the work that other insects and the wind also did.

Because the bees in their skeps discouraged disturbance, the bee yard was always a holy and quiet place. A weary homesteader could leave her hot kitchen behind and venture out to sit on the little stool near the hives. She would bend her head and listen to the hum from inside the skep and fan her face with her apron. These house-women were as busy as the bees, and they recognized their kinship.

This respect and familiarity led to the custom of "telling the bees." People believed that any important event in the family had to be reported to the bees, or they would feel insulted and leave the garden forever. Marriage had to be reported, with an appropriate amount of detail about the dress and the cake. Births generally required less detail, but the amount of joy and blessing was always reflected in the way the hives reacted.

But deaths were always the most important event to announce, especially the death of the head of the household. Bees are sensitive to mood, you know, and when their family is in mourning, they understand the sadness and confusion. If they are not informed in a rather formal way, it can disturb them enough to join their wild cousins in the woods.

Those pony girls were taught hive respect at an early age and will often stand closer to their bee deepyard to whisper about a gift from their grandma or hurt feelings from a careless word. The bees like the girls and are delighted when one of them attaches a fluttering paper that holds a colorfully drawn picture to the back of the hive boxes. They are short-lived, these gifts, for they are diminished by the rain and the wind, leaving colorful scraps in the meadow, which the ponies sometimes eat. The bees have no opinion of the ponies but are grateful that the fence between their sharp hooves is both stout and electrified. This keeps the bees safe and the ponies indifferent.

The bees are almost all female, and they know the ways of the lands around them. Since they and their wings are small, they never travel farther than about three miles in any one direction, so they know that territory very well indeed.

Instructed in the delicate diplomacy of human and hive, we have come to this bee yard with our own news and to make a request. The girls are inside the house now, eating thick slices of lemon cake and drinking milk. The ponies are uninterested in us, and so we are alone with tens of thousands of working bees who would rather not be disturbed.

Because we are quiet and move slowly, the bees continue to fly in and out of the wooden boxes, going in with full saddlebags and exiting with keen enthusiasm to find more pollen. Each colony has guard bees at the door, and as we approach the yellow hive on the end of the row, three bees meet us, flying back and forth in a zigzag pattern in front of our faces. We stand very still. They won't recognize our faces, for we are not their tenders. But they may understand that we don't pose a threat and allow us closer.

With a swift turn, they go back to the top of the hive and pass their news onto the other workers. We have been spotted, but we are not bears nor mischievous children. Then they return to their guard duties, satisfied.

We are here to relate the news we gathered among the hags and the maenads, words we were given to share. We bend down near the entrance to the hive—the little wooden porch—and some of us sit on the ground, careful of tired bees that may not have the strength to reach home. One by one, each of us whispers the story we have come to tell. One story is shared about the desert. Another bit of news is about a broken shoe that had to be repaired. On and on they flow and the bees seem glad of so much news from outside their small world. They perch on the sides and tops of the hive boxes, fanning their wings to cool themselves and their sisters. When the last news is shared and we rise to stretch ourselves, the workers fly up and around our heads, watching us with their glistening eyes. We know that this is the time to ask the favor and we do.

To the south of where the bee yard stands, there is a low hollow hill that is often visited by the young foragers. A meadow with flowers lies at its foot and a small brook runs into the hill and out of it again.

Hollow hills are peculiar things, rare but not impossible to find. Some are natural, their guts dissolved through the action of water and time. Others were constructed by long-ago humans as a place to leave their celebrated dead. The third kind is the most intriguing, and that is what resides here near the pasture and bee yard. It is the home of otherworldly folk who choose to live away from the harshness of the summer sun and the chill of winter winds. They venture out sometimes to see how the outside world is conducting itself and usually come back unimpressed or annoyed.

There are generally ways for outside folks to enter hollow hills. There is a crevice where a certain word can be spoken to open a door. Sometimes there is a cavelet whose entrance is covered with evergreen bushes and thorny weeds. Most people don't bother with them unless there is a rumor—always unfounded—of treasure. Then come the pickaxes and shovels and the hill mightily resists this intrusion. After all, the treasure that lies in this cave is not what those miscreants are looking for—and the people inside aren't interested in what the outsiders want. The hill and its insiders do all they can to keep their laws and to avoid unpleasant contact with unpleasant humans. Sadly for all, those are the humans they usually encounter.

It is this hill we have come to visit. And, if we are lucky, to encounter the ones who live within.

We bow, as is our custom, as the bees circle around our heads.

Please, will you lead us into the hill?

Their flying becomes frenetic and they move to the center of the bee yard. Bees from other colonies fly into the cloud, and they seem to be in council. We have asked for a big favor, it seems, and we prepare ourselves for a refusal. There may be other ways to enter the mountain, and we may be able to find another entrance. As quickly as the council-flight had begun, it disperses, and the workers go back to foraging and guarding. Information was taken into the hive bodies and consultation was taking place.

Chapter 7

This is the way of hive minds, whether bee or ant. Every member has responsibility for the health and safety of the group, and any decision must be undertaken with this as the paramount importance. The workers do not go into the main hive body to consult the queen. She is the mother of all and is fed and tended as she goes about her life's work of laying the next generations, but she is not the boss. Our request ripples through the mind of the collective in ways humans do not yet understand. There may be dancing—we see some of that exhibited on the top of each hive—but however the means, the information is distributed and answers ripple back in response. It is finally agreed that scouts will in fact honor our bold request.

The entire process takes no more than a few minutes. The bees return to work once more, except for a handful of bees that hover between us and the hill and then begin a slow meandering flight. It takes us a moment to read these signs and to respond in kind. We take off at a steady pace and follow the bees about a mile to the hill.

They disappear for a moment, and we wonder if they have done what they agreed, led us to the hill but not inside it. We feel a sharp disappointment. We look around for our scouts, and they are nowhere to be seen. We take out our water bottles and drink and begin to think about our next move.

Quite close by, we can hear the crystal sound of a rivulet of water falling into a pool. We creep nearer the sound, and there we see the bee scouts, hovering over the small pool. It is a faeryscape of fern, glinting water, and flowers bobbing their heads over the reflecting pool. We laugh with the delight of it and feel, again and always, the enchantment that fills our world, enchantment we sometimes forget. We apologize to the bees and thank them for this perfect vision, but we see they have moved on to a crack in the hillside that was probably carved out by the rivulet over countless years. On closer inspection, we see a gap between a ragged tree and some bramble bushes with green berries on their arching canes. The bees are floating there, anxious to get back to their foraging work, waiting for our slow human brains to catch on.

This is the way in.

Our body language must have changed, for the bees darted away, leaving us here to figure it out. It takes us a few minutes until we realize that if we skinny ourselves past the thorny canes and lean into the crack behind the ragged tree, we might be able to squeeze through. The smallest of us volunteers, and we see that the skinnying technique seems to work as she disappears behind the tree.

Come on. It's big enough. There's plenty of room.

We leave our packs on the ground. The narrow passage is deceptive and is much easier to navigate than it looks from outside. We have no idea what we will encounter here, and the adventure of this passageway may be the only adventure forthcoming. As we wiggle through, we feel carvings under the hands that are guiding us along and realize the earthy wall has given way to a stone-lined corridor. We whisper to each other, our fingers tracing the swirls of the carved patterns. We freeze in our journey through and fall into the spell of the walls. Circles, leaf patterns, chevrons, lozenges—all dance under our fingertips.

We don't know how long we have been standing there, tracing the carvings in the stone, but we feel drugged by the activity and realize we have been hanging in that corridor far longer than we thought. Someone coughs and another makes a little groaning sound because we have been standing so long in one place. We finally begin to move forward again, realizing this was some trickery of the hollow hill, wondering how many people come in alone and never make it past the beautiful, treacherous walls.

We can see a little now, for we are coming to an open place. What little light from the outside has soon left us in the passageway, and our time with the carvings was completely in the dark. We move in twilight now and the corridor has widened so that we can walk almost normally. There was always a chance that the cleft in the mountain would simply end partway in and we'd have to reverse our steps back into the meadow. But it seems this hill is at least partly hollow, and our excitement begins to grow again.

The corridor abruptly dumps us into a long room. We stretch ourselves and look around us. This place is like nothing we have seen in our travels, and it is thick with magic, the same sort of enchantment that embraced us in the passageway. The walls are very high and the ceiling far away. If we had thought a hollow hill would be like a dug-out cave, with the ends of roots in the walls and clods of dirt on the floor, we find ourselves much mistaken. This is a chamber, appointed with all that is needed to live well and happily.

The light is soft but certainly bright enough to see, and it comes from sconces on the wall and pendulous lamps that hang on braided chains from the far ceiling. The quality of the light is odd. It is unlike the brightness of midnight, nor is it like the full Moon. It is most like the golden light that falls from the west at the end of an autumn day. It is peculiar to see it coming from these lighting fixtures, and that adds to the overall oddness of the place.

There are sections of sleeping and reclining alcoves along the walls, and these are covered with bedclothes and hangings in fabrics we don't know. Some are sheer, others thick and soft looking. The divans inside the alcoves look tempting and warm. We are all suddenly taken with an overpowering urge to lie down and sleep. But we are wary now and only share our yawns as we take little jars from our pockets and sip the water we brought in with us.

There doesn't seem to be anyone around, and so we wander a bit to keep ourselves awake and to satisfy our curiosity. We walk carefully, noting the floor in front of us and keeping our eyes open for trickery. We remember the old folk tales, the stories from the Brothers Grimm, of Charles Perrault and Madame d'Aulnoy, and from all the old wives in every village and township. Plus, we can feel the dense magic in the air all around us, perfumed like poppies, redolent with charms and glamours.

We are being as careful as we know how to be.

At one end of the chamber is a raised dais, covered in rugs and backed with a tapestry. Woven into the tapestry, we recognize two of the creatures we met in the desert—the dragon-woman and the bird-woman—and we ponder the interconnectedness of this pilgrimage, not for the first time. Do they live here? Visit here? Or do they live in the dreams of the people who do inhabit this place?

On the dais, perched on the thick carpets, is a low chair, carved from heavy wood. The carvings match the ones on the wall, and we suspect they are one of the sources of the insistent magic. A cushion is on the seat of the chair, but it doesn't have a back. It is utterly unthronelike and yet seems to be exactly that.

We wander back the way we have come and arrive at an area of small tables and more heavy chairs. The tables are covered in more of the scrumptious cloth, and each table has different foods piled high on it. The food isn't on plates or serving dishes but simply piled onto the cloth. We lean in to look at the pile, and the food doesn't seem real. There are bunches of orange grapes, piles of black strawberries with glistening silver seeds. There are purple pears and boiled blue eggs. The bread looks as carved as the chairs and the butter is glistening gold.

So many of the places we encounter in our workaday world bear the same imprint. Objects seem real enough until you touch them and they crumble. Food looks edible until you put it in your mouth and realize there is no nutrition and the taste is unnatural. This hollow hill is no different but less subtle. One of us picks up the bunch of fat orange grapes, and we see that each grape is shaped like a pumpkin with ridges in the sides. Some of them even have the jolly face of a jack-o'-lantern.

We think this must be our lesson here—that things are often not what they seem, that beauty is not always truth and comfort can sometimes be a way to keep us from our true selves. That seems an important thing to have learned and is easily integrated, and so we move back toward the entry point of the passageway.

It is then we hear a sound at the other far end of the room. A flute or is it a harp? We are relieved that there may be something in this adventure a little more meaty and instructive, but we are strangely disappointed not to be venturing back out to the pretty meadow with its flowers, ponies, and bees. The sound is, of course, charming, captivating, and we do not hesitate to move in that direction. We expect to see another dais, perhaps with a fey orchestra or a four-piece insect ensemble. But there is only a planter box filled with soil and herbs and an old-fashioned baby carriage. The music is everywhere—it permeates everything—and seems to be coming from the carriage. One of us grabs the high handle and gently turns the carriage around so that the occupant can be seen.

It is a baby with hair the color of the sea. A perfectly normal child who is smiling and gurgling. She is not surprised to see us and reaches her chubby arms into the air in the universal sign of all babies to be picked up. As one of us reaches in, she laughs brightly, a not very human nor baby sort of laugh. We are immediately on guard, but she seems unmoved by our suspicion.

She speaks then in an accent we don't know, but her language is ours. Her voice is that of an adult, and it is disconcerting in that cheeky face.

It has taken you so long to arrive! We have set up everything here as you would like. Do you like? Is it familiar?

We're not sure how to respond, but she only laughs and continues.

We haven't gotten it quite right, have we? That's typical—we don't go into the outer lands often and we lose track of you and your ways. But now you are here and you are very welcome. No one has been in this hall for so long, and we feared you had forgotten us. Or were remembering our old times of enmity and war.

Forget that now! There is much to do and much to teach you before you return to the outside. We are pleased with your gift of these fragrant herbs, and we think we can come together in council to discuss our worlds—inner and outer—and how we can ameliorate some of what you have done.

Will you dine with me? The baby gestures toward one of the far tables. We shake our heads but we do smile. *Ah, I see you do remember us! There is wisdom there that you have gleaned from your wise women. We honor them.*

With that, the baby gestures again and we sit on the low wooden seats. She claps her hands and laughs again, and into our heads come the visions She wishes for us to see.

It is the widest of trance journeys, and we give in to it with no reservations. First, we see the prairies of the world as we saw them early in our sojourn. The sacred grasslands and all that dwell within them and above them. The forests are next. Mile after mile of thick trunks, of mother trees that shield their young. We stand on the great road of mycelium that brings our spirits throughout the world.

We see the mushroom-shaped clouds and the burning rivers. We see starving babies and their gaunt mamas. We watch as the nuclear meltdown rages and wolves roam the empty spaces. Humans are locked into their machines—cars, phones, cubicles for work. We watch ourselves become less human, desperate, terrified, furious.

Now we are sitting quietly beside our families, families of blood and families of heart. We sit in thoughtful circles, and we learn from the elders and the children and from the shared experiences of all who sit in this solemn and enchanted place.

We hold the hands of the birthing mother, the weeping child, the dying grandmother. We hold each other's hands, and that grasp is immediate and everlasting. We hold the past, the future, and the present, and we connect ourselves to the Primal Mothers and the Babies, all of whom teach us. We reach across space and time, and nothing is impossible for us as our ancestors, our descendants, and the Divines stand with us.

We sit lost in this teaching, our eyes closed, our breath held. And when we open our eyes, we are sitting outside the hollow hill, near our backpacks and bags. We are alone—except for the bees that watch us with their glistening eyes. We hear Her voice as we turn to follow our scouts back to the meadow and the bee yard and the ponies.

You have spent much time with the Beloved Mothers, my kindred. But now you must consider the Beloved Children, the Sacred Girl Child and all She sees and gives to the world. Love your ancestors and also love your descendants, for all the children of the earth are your descendants whether you birthed them or not. You are here to protect and honor them, to ease their burdens as you can, and to hold their futures as clearly as your own in your service to the Primal Mothers and All Their Sisters.

Perceptions

We aren't used to thinking generationally these days unless we have children or grandchildren or are caretaking aging elders. We are encouraged to think for today and maybe until the weekend but rarely further than that. To think generationally should give us pause when we make any long-term decision. As citizens, we should certainly encourage planners, developers, and elected officials to think long-term—not until the next election but into the next decade, the next century. Think of the things that now have to be undone or redone because our ancestors didn't have as much information as we do and dammed up streams that we are now setting free, clear-cut forests that we are regrowing, and used up resources we now understand are precious and rarer than we ever knew.

Bees remind us that humans also bear responsibility for each other, and we thrive when we can practice something like hive life in our neighborhoods and communities. Bring generational thinking to the table in your kitchen, in your spiritual circle, at your town council or state legislature. Encourage long vision in whatever way fits your communication style—storytelling, letters, podcasts, blogs. Sing the songs of years to come and the descendants who will inherit what we and the other ancestors leave behind for them. We can take responsibility for this vision and do our best to make it so.

Chapter 8
WARRIOR. LOVER. LAWGIVER.

We carry, mile by mile, the weight of expectation, of responsibility, of personal and cultural history. With each movement into new territory, we are dragged back and weighed down by dense baggage, some of which is not our own. In our struggles with agency, we have taken on this baggage from others we have deemed too weak to carry it themselves. We are helpers, each one of us, and we are strong as young oxen. Our compassion is coupled with arrogance—the arrogance that leads us to foolishly overburden ourselves to prove our worth, our value.

You and I are not young oxen, and we never have been. We are human folk of various ages, in various stages of our lives. These pathworkings we undertake in our pilgrimage will show us possibilities for dropping some of the baggage, for relieving ourselves of some of the burden.

Our work here is to reproduce this powerful initiatory rite of passage. One by one, we will undertake this initiation, this stripping away of what no longer serves us. In the places we have journeyed so far, we have had each other's company, which has often been a valuable reminder that we are not alone. This place is different. This is one of the few solo encounters in our wanderings. Each of us will be alone and helpless, and that is the point.

This is the oldest resurrection literature. It is a reframing of the Sumerian myth that is called the Descent of Inanna, and it has been used in modern times as a pathworking designed to sharpen our encounter with Other as well as Self. It introduces the theme of a dying and resurrecting god, one that is easily seen in agricultural societies where crops are planted, tended, harvested, and replanted in the next season.

THE JOURNEY

We are preparing ourselves for this descent because we are aware of the history as well as the significance of what we are doing. We talk so much about shadow work, but so few people actually come to grips with what that means. Tomorrow's encounter will bring us face-to-face with so many things we have stuffed down and ignored in our lives. To clear out that emotional clutter and those memories of trauma that we still carry in our bodies is an act that must be done for our spiritual, emotional, and mental health. We carry all that to our detriment. With the goal of freedom and divine connection as our hearts' desire, we are taking this step to clear the way—and to ready ourselves for what is to come.

We are doing all the things we know how and begin sitting together and setting intentions. There is much discussion of the possibilities as well as safeguards for potential hazards. That is the hardest because being uncomfortable is certainly part of where we are, and using that discomfort as a tool to dig into who we are is vital. Fear is also a component of our sojourn because fear is a necessary safeguard, but it is also a block and an anchor around our necks. When is fear appropriate to keep us safe, and when is it an unconscious reaction to the myriad perceived dangers that aren't dangers at all? We have been told throughout our lives that being small and meek is a safe way to keep dangerous attention away from us. But suppressing our feral natures—choosing meekness and niceness—doesn't change either our personal or the cultural status quo. When we observe and experience the overarching dominance that patriarchy excels in, we understand that being small and tame has never made us safe. Sooner or later, we must stand up and speak the truth.

After our intentions, we do a run-through of what will happen in the Descent, as well as the Ascent when the work is complete. We know there are gatekeepers who will demand sacrifices from us, level by level, until we are naked and vulnerable. We understand that the destination of the Descent is to come into direct contact with our shadow, with the demons that pursue us and with new tools for our journey. All of that seems very vague and poetic, even when we breathe deeply and close our eyes to imagine it. There is a frisson of fear that ripples through us, and we hold it close to us, protectively. The uncertainty and the fear are part of this, and we acknowledge that to ourselves and to each other.

Then each of us spends time alone. Not much can be said about that. It is private and fierce and preparatory. Each of us takes the amount of time needed. As we finish our prayers and dreams, we take a bath or shower to bless our bodies and cleanse them, too. Now we are ready. Now we will sleep.

We travel next morning to the entrance of a cave. This entrance is not a vine-covered hole in the side of the mountain as we have encountered in other stops along the way. It is a manufactured entryway and has been used many times, by many people. The doorway has a carved wooden door that isn't hinged but slides to one side on a track. It stands open, waiting for us.

We need only a moment of grounding, of focusing, and we are ready. We will not go as a group. That has been a great comfort in other places, but we are informed that these personal journeys must be undertaken one by one. No shaded area protects us from the sun, and we are resolved about the heat and bright light. One by one, we descend. You go first. You lead the way.

You step into the opening and disappear into the darkness. You are wearing the best clothes that you own and have chosen each piece for its symbolic power and its beauty. You stood before the mirror this morning and nodded your approval at your choices.

It takes a few moments for your eyes to adjust, and you relish the coolness inside the entrance. Soon you can see a short stairway in front of you, a stairway that ends in a decorated doorway. You are careful on the steps and arrive at the doorway. You wait, wondering if you should open the door or knock or even call out. The door opens on its own and you walk inside. As you do, the door closes behind you.

There is a soft light on the small landing, enough to see a long mirror against one wall. Ahead lies another staircase with a little railing. You turn to the mirror and see that your head covering—a pretty scarf that you borrowed from your friend—is illuminated more than the rest of your reflected image. You think of your friend, grateful for the scarf and sad to let it go. But you know the story and remove the wrapped scarf, fold it, and set it at the base of the mirror. The mirror darkens, and you turn to the staircase.

There is a slight curve, and you descend a dozen or so steps. There you find the same setting as the first door. You face the mirror and see your necklace and bracelets highlighted by the strange light. You take them off and set them down, then remove your earrings so that you have on no jewelry. As before, the soft light blinks out and the mirror and the landing are darkened but still navigable.

Twelve steps down to the next level, and you are more curious than afraid. The mirror lights up your shoes and you shake your head. *Shoes? Okay, shoes.* You place them at the mirror, but the light continues to shine on your socks. With shoes and socks removed, you find pleasure in the coolness of the floor.

Twelve more steps that continue the curve from before. The same door opens at your approach, and you stand quietly while the door slides open. The mirror shows your leather belt. It is an old favorite of yours, the only one that felt comfortable and buckled easily. You like the buckle, too, which you had gotten separately from the belt. It is a silver one, heavy and plain. You sigh as you unbuckle it and roll it into a tight coil before depositing it on the floor. Your loose clothes float around you and the light dims.

Twelve more steps, still curving. The door is open this time and the mirror's light shines as soon as you step in. You are completely illuminated from shoulders to ankles. You take off the lightweight cotton cover-up that you had added to your wardrobe at the last minute. You move your mobile phone into an inner pocket—it seems silly to have brought it, but you rarely go anywhere without it. Off comes the wrap, and you drop it on the floor. The mirror goes dark.

Wearing only a sleeveless dress, you go down twelve more steps, being careful of your bare feet slipping as you descend. The door is the same as before, of course. You are a little bored now and want to get on with it. The door opens, you go in and face the mirror. There's really only one thing left.

But you are wrong about that. The mirror illuminates the dress except for an odd dark patch at your pocket. You turn this way and that and the patch moves with you. You finally understand that the dress has to go but you are to keep the phone. *Ridiculous*, you think. *There's no coverage down here, and I have it turned off anyway. Why not just keep it in the pocket of the dress?*

Once more you dutifully take off your final garment and the mirror turns to shadows. But you stand there, looking at your body reflected so gently. You play with your hair, fluffing it out. You turn sideways and look at your silhouette. Then back around to the front. You don't often think of your body, not really. It isn't perfect and you are well aware of that. You were always described as "scrawny" when you were growing up, or "little" because you are short as well as small-boned. But you were never an acceptable, pixie-ish girl. Instead you were always awkward, insect-like. You shrug now, having survived middle school.

Sharp tears sting your eyes then, remembering those hard years. You had felt totally, utterly, alone. Friendless and bookish, not included in others' activities. For a moment, you are there again, then you remember the journey and what it means to be free, to find a mother much different than your own. You cast another look at the mirror, pick up your phone, and return to the twisting staircase.

Twelve more steps. You do the math quickly in your head as you descend and wonder how far down you are. The walls seem very solid, not at all crumbly or cracking. You are surprised when there is another door. Surely you have given all away? What can you possibly give up here? As before, the door opens and you step inside. The mirror brings up its soft light and there, in your hand, is your answer.

Your phone. Your lifeline to the rest of the world. Your friends, your contacts, even your banking information. You realize that your entire life is in that little plastic box, and for a second you are frozen. You are looking at the phone in the mirror and not seeing the rest of your body. The light in the mirror glows brighter, and you move the phone from one hand to the other and the light follows it.

You look down at its face. The screen holds a picture of your cats, and you note that the charge on the battery is still good.

No bars, no connectivity. You try to scroll past the page and nothing moves. Your cats are there. Those good babies. They are literally the only thing you have left to you. The information inside feels suddenly irrelevant. Only the cats, your truest friends, are there. How can you give them up? You feel a rising panic. The kitties. Your kitties.

The light on the mirror is very bright on the phone and the hand holding it, and there is also a low grating sound, a growl. You are stubborn about this now, protective, and shake your head. The sound grows louder. You can't do it. You will never get to the Great Below—and you don't care. Let the next one find you here standing in front of the mirror, clutching your phone to your naked breast. You don't care, you aren't giving it up, aren't giving them up. Your mind flies to the conversation the evening before. You are searching for any helpful tools they might have discussed, something you might have missed. You remember the gentle but firm voice of one of your companions. *We can do this. I know we can.* The remembered friend had reached out her hand and touched you. *I know you can, love.*

The growl is fierce now as you remember that tenderness, as you remember your friend. You look at your beautiful cats and know this was the last gate, and you are ready to go into this shadowland, free and unencumbered.

You set the phone at the base of the mirror and the light goes out, the growling ceases. Instead there is a sort of tuneless humming, not quite a song, not quite not a song. The mirror again glows softly, bathing your body in exquisite rosy light. You look at yourself, your whole self, and you feel love and tenderness mist over you, the sort of tenderness you have rarely been given your whole life, even by the cats. You smile at your reflection, nod your head. You bow three times to the rosy glow and your strong, beloved self, and you turn to face the door and the darkness of the Great Below.

This is indeed the last gate of the Descent, and you know you will face twelve steps. Beyond that, you have no idea. The sweet humming and soft light follow you down the last steps, then they abruptly stop, and you are in darkness.

As the first person into the Great Below, you find a corridor that ends in a room with a small table with benches on each of the four sides. Strangely, there is a window in one wall, and you can't fathom how that is possible when you are so deeply inside the earth. It may be some trick, an illusion that adds something to the work you are called to do in this place.

You take a seat at the table, which seems the obvious thing to do in the situation. On the table is a crockery pitcher of water and a cluster of small cups in the same material. In this shadow parlor—there is one for each of us—you are overcome with a heavy sleepiness and put your head down on your arms. You fall immediately to sleep. It is a drugged sort of sleep, as though you have taken a powerful medication. It is hard to know how long the sleeping lasts but the dreams are intense, colorful, a review of the worst and most challenging moments of your life.

You relive your loneliness, the violence you experienced more than once, the rape, the abuse, the humiliation, the shame, and the guilt of a life lived under harsh systems of oppression with no obvious means of escape. With each segment of dream, your body jerks, trying to wake you. But the heaviness prevails and you return to the ruthless analysis and review. Tears course down your cheeks and dampen your arms.

After a time, this horror simply ends and the dreams change abruptly. The colors are lighter and brighter, the scenes are ones of care and delight and love, most of which you had long forgotten. You are sitting at your grandmother's table, kicking your legs and waiting for cookies—your favorite cookies—to come out of the oven. Your grandmother's smile is small and a little coy, just like your own.

Another scene shows you in high school, in your bedroom alone, reading a book. There is a scratching at the door, and you reluctantly get off the bed to open it. In waddles the family cat, a fat orange cat named Rusty. You squat down and scoop him up in your arms—oof, he is heavy and a little surly. But you are his favorite even if he shows it by digging his claws into your shoulder. You go to the chair by the window and sit, letting him slide into your lap. You try to reach your book on the foot of the bed. Every time you reach over, Rusty growls and wags his tail. You finally give up and look out the window as Rusty settles into your lap and falls asleep, purring.

Story after story plays out in the dreamworld. After the love and tenderness has healed so many places in your sad soul, the dreams change again and return to some of the terrors from before. Some of them—but certainly not all—are viewed with different eyes. You see the other lonely girl that sat at your table and remember her smile. The weird boy with greasy hair who followed you around seems less a threat now and more a kindred spirit with no self-confidence and few social skills. On and on, you see some of these haunting memories with new understanding. Even the violent episodes can be approached without the lingering shame and guilt—you now know you were not the cause of any of that and bear no responsibility for the violent actions of others.

The stories play around and around, each viewing bringing new wisdom, new insight into the pain you have carried for so long. You remember those moments of perfect happiness—even the grumpy cat—and you will not forget them again. The shame, guilt, and loss have softer edges now, and you discover you can hold a place of forgiveness, even for yourself.

You wake with a start and stand up quickly. You are panting with the effort but are as quickly awake as you fell quickly asleep. You look around the room, expecting to see the characters from your life's story there. But you are alone.

Looking down at the table, you spy the pitcher of water and pour yourself a drink. You drink one, then another, and stop after a third. The room feels close and stuffy, and you go to the peculiar window and look out. A sunset is blooming in the west, and you reach to open the window, which slides to one side with little effort. A gentle breeze cools your brow and lifts the hair from your forehead and neck. You no longer know if it is real or not. This time in pilgrimage has given you more resilience than before and a vivid imagination that zips through time and space. A window that offers a cooling wind and a view of the setting sun from deep inside a mountain is hardly a stretch. Which you do, stretching your arms high above your head and then bending at the waist to touch the floor. You shut the window and have another cup of water before turning to the door.

You wonder briefly about the others and about your clothes. You don't think a thing about your phone as you return down that narrow corridor to begin your Ascent from the Great Below. The last door is now the first one, and all the doors on your journey upward are open for you. You climb the stairs to the first landing.

The mirror shows you a glowing reflection of herself, beautiful and strong. You pick up your phone and look at your cats. Remembering old Rusty, you turn to the open door. Looking back at your reflection, you see that it is good.

Up twelve steps and on to the next small landing. Still glowing in the mirror, you put on your dress and smooth it over your hips. You tuck the phone into your pocket and make for the door.

The process repeats itself landing after landing as you retrieve your cover-up, your belt, your socks and shoes, your jewelry, and finally your scarf. You pause before this last mirror and tuck your hair under the silky fabric. You look into the mirror for a long time, seeing replays of the cat, the grandmother, the sunset. You can almost smell the cookies.

The mirror darkens as you watch, and you know it is time to go. You have descended to the Great Below (which might better be called the Great Within) and know you have done the work that you needed to finish before the next challenge, before the seasons shifts.

The rest of us had also gone into the dark cave mouth, one at a time. The door slid closed after each one and slid open again when the next sojourner was expected. Each of us followed the same pattern as the one before, ending in the darkness, alone and naked. Each went through a curtained archway and into a corridor. Each encounter was different, and each was earth-shaking for the one who experienced it.

You step to the final carved doorway, which slides back silently. You stride into the burning sunset of the Great Above and wait for the rest of the seekers to join you.

Perceptions

As darkness begins to settle on the year, on the land, and on your heart, subtly at first, remember the lessons of the staircase. When we are called to give something up, when we are called to sacrifice a comfort or conserve our use of resources like water and electricity, let's remember the lessons of the staircase as we descend it, leaving behind the things we think we can never be without. Darkness of night and endarkening of the seasons doesn't mean we are bereft of what we need. Darkness is a time and place of contemplation, of healing, of germination, and of gestation. Remember those who are not so privileged as you and learn the difference between charity and justice. As Inanna leads us into the sure and empty passage of our personal underworld, may your wisdom and intuition soften your heart and your hands and offer you the grace to let go what must be set aside or left behind.

Part 2

THE DARKENING: SUMMER SOLSTICE TO WINTER SOLSTICE

We have walked so many roads, tripped, stumbled, fallen, and helped each other up, all in our search for places where we can encounter the Divines of old. We have supped with monsters, drowned in cold water, lost ourselves in hollow hills of memory and deceit.

Here the roads end where we began, on the longest and darkest night, this perfect solstice. The sky above us is palest blue, and chubby clouds veil the sun for a moment and then scurry on about their business. We have come here to rest and reflect on all we have seen—and all we have been—thus far on our journey. We rest our spirits and bodies for the ordeal work yet to come. For we have arrived at the turning point of the journey, and from here we turn ourselves over to the times of testing and, if we are lucky, reclamation and communion. Leaving this gentle, safe place will not mirror our frenzied escape from the manicured garden, hearts pierced with elf-shot. This is a reasoned pathway, one we welcome in our hunger for this feral church, this experience of divine love beyond liturgy and holy books, beyond buildings and dogma. No stained-glass windows, no font, no pulpit. Only the sky and the sea, the desert and the prairie, the bayou and the crag. Our baptism will not be a sprinkle of tepid water but a roar of flame. No priest stands between us and Her, for none could survive such a place.

This time we have some inkling of what is to come, and it will end, as all things end, in death. But if we have done well, it also finishes with rebirth, with resurrection. No substitute of lamb or sweet smoke or sacred son. We are the sacrifice and we are the grace.

Chapter 9
EATING THE APPLE

This journey takes us into the heat and humidity of the swamplands, into the heart of Cajun country. The food and company will delight us, and we will meet an unexpected vision of the Goddess, one that seems familiar and feels new, too.

THE JOURNEY

We are having a true Gulf Coast treat tonight. We have our bowl and soup spoon ready as gumbo is ladled out of a steaming pot. Shrimp on top and chunks of okra and bell pepper swim in the richest gravy. Bend over your bowl to get a good whiff and watch your glasses fog up just so you can get that smell. That is real gumbo and it is heaven on earth.

After the gumbo, we help cover a table with layers of newspaper, and a garbage bag of crawfish, shrimp, corn on the cob, and potatoes is dumped in the middle. A roll of paper towels is passed around and we each pull off a long string and stuff it in our laps between our thighs. It is messy eating, and each face gets smeared like we have taste buds all around our mouths. Our hands get greasy because there must be some taste buds there, too. In between all that eating, we swig ice cold bottles of beer and red cups of Coke. If we're lucky, there might be some of the local Cajun hooch. But you have to be careful with that, because it will hurt you if you think you're too clever. Goes down rough and stays rough, that bayou moonshine.

We had met with some Cajun friends a couple of days ago, and they filled us in on swamps and bayous. They also fed us fried alligator tail and that local high-alcohol drink that is made of bark. It was very strong but not very tasty. The gumbo, though, and the crawdad boil, that taste kept on going all night long.

To be with a group of people who love to share food is a blessing that we don't appreciate enough. It is rare in our weight-conscious world to be with people who love to eat and aren't shy about it or guilty about it, not being shamed by a basic joy that too many of us have squelched for far too long. Our Cajun friends want us to taste the best of their table and their culture, and they were proud of it and easy in their hospitality. After the marathon of supper, we all clear away the mess only to find it is simple to wad up the newspaper with the grease, the paper towels, and the corncobs and haul it out to the compost bin. The shells of crawdad and shrimp are bagged for the freezer for stock later on. Beer bottles get rinsed and into the glass recycling tub to go out to the recycling center when somebody is headed that way. The gumbo bowls and spoons are washed in a pan of hot, sudsy water before the rice can turn to glue. All that is left are the red cups, but they are empty, so we refill them and go out on the porch. Somebody turns the porch lights on and the bug zapper, too. There aren't enough chairs, so a bunch of us sit on the edge of the porch, our feet dangling down and kicking back and forth in time to the music.

We get some stories now and that wild music that the region is rightly famous for. The little squeezebox gets it all started, then a fiddle and another fiddle, and a guitar. All the instruments look well used, and the sound that comes together on that porch is the work of skilled hands and wild spirits. We step out onto the yard to jump around to the music. Sometimes there is a break—either for one instrument or the whole group—and more drinks come out. There is a big plate of fried alligator tail, too, with rounds of dense bread and some butter. In between the playing and singing and eating, our friends tell stories and dark jokes. We learn about their forebears and their other kin, about the mischief they got up to and the tragedy that too often visits itself on the people of the region. We eat, listen, drink, and dance like we have no bones in our bodies.

Music is a funny thing. There are all kinds of music all over the world, and most cultures have signature musical styles and instruments. There's usually an instrument with strings, some that make sound by blowing through or over them, and something percussive to keep the rhythm. Some cultures also have an instrument that has keys, and some have instruments that are a combination of things.

But the way in which the culture and environment is situated affects both the instrument and the ways in which it is played and combined with others, which is where the real differences lie. It is particularly fascinating to look at modern revivals of ancient instruments and musical styles. We seem to have a visceral understanding of our ancestors when we hear these simple instruments played by skilled hands.

Music is the breathwork of cultures and has remarkable power. Hearing the diversity of voice and instrument can help us understand cultures that feel so different from our own. It isn't only the "exotic" sounds of lands far away but also listening intently to the music of our most recent forebears that can be most satisfying. Our great-uncle in Pittsburgh loves Oktoberfest beer-barrel polkas. Our Appalachian grandmother loved old-style country music. Those cousins that we don't know well are shape-note singers and their children are jazz musicians. All these sounds bring us a flavor of who they were and who we are.

We connect with these divine music bringers and happily turn our attentions back to the porchlight frolic. Sometime later, we all turn in for the night, to wake only a few hours later to the smell of coffee brewing and eggs and bacon frying.

This goes on for a couple of days, and in between the feasting and the jollification, we hear stories of the spirits of this place—the ghosts of lawless men, the little lights that float on the water, the wild boars, the holy ones who seem to favor the bayous, and the peculiar folks that call them home. We are especially touched to learn of their devotion to the Blessed Virgin. The celebration of Her Assumption—which is when She ascended into heaven without dying—is also the Acadians' national holiday.

During the daylight hours, we wander around the property to get acquainted with the plants and trees and to see any local animals that might be brave enough to show themselves to us. It turns out the local insects, snakes, opossums, and raccoons are as bold as can be, and we learn to carry stout sticks with us on those walks. But the view across the bayou is so beautiful, it's worth the vigilance, and we soon get used to scanning the vicinity to see who we are sharing the space with. The insects are harder—they dive-bomb us from above, below, and every possible direction.

Sunset and sunrise are especially moving. The sun rises through the tangle of trees and undergrowth, shooting rays of brilliance onto the dewy leaves and into our faces. The sunset happens right into the bayou, and the frogs and gators sing a song of lust and exultation as the sunfire lowers itself into the water. It is the color of lava for a few moments, and we can imagine a race of frogs that not only lives in it but sings of their resilience and power in such an impossible situation.

That sets right with us, the exultation and the resilience. We gather in their songs of desire and press them deeply into our souls, into our feral selves, adding another layer, another petal to the gathering-in of all that makes us whole.

Every day we find ourselves around an odd apparition in the front yard, over on one side of the porch. It looks like a bathtub that has been sunk into the ground on the tap end, and inside its porcelain arch is a statue of the Blessed Virgin Mary. It has traces of the original blue and white robes, and She has a snake curling around Her feet. But someone has changed Her traditional colors and done some fancy eye makeup so that she stands before us in a dusty dark pink color, and Her veil and shawl are black. The snake is curling around Her ankle, not stomped down but peaceful. Mary's gaze is not demure or downcast. She looks directly at each of us, and there is that trick of the eyes where it looks like Her gaze follows us wherever we move. Her look is open and curious but discerning, and we know She is quite aware of the level of partying we have done in the last few days.

Our friend explains that it is half a bathtub and that his mama had done the painting project. His mama was a well-known "outsider artist," but she has been dead for fourteen years now. He tears up when he talks about her, but then he laughs when he remembers that his mama did the painting in the middle of one of those wild parties and she had been drinking a big cup of good 'shine. She said the Blessed Mother had come to share her cup and told her what to paint. Then our friend slapped his leg, poured a libation from his red cup, turned, and walked away.

It is decided that one of our friends will take us out tomorrow and we can see for ourselves what these places are like. We are warned about sunscreen and bug spray and what we should wear. There is a lot of talk about shoes, but we have gone too far into all this sojourning to have anything on our feet that we can't use to stomp, to kick, or to run. We feel a little proud of that, too.

Next morning we head out to the dock and board the boat. We are given a basket with sandwiches and fruit and one of those old red and white Playmate coolers full of cold drinks. We have a satchel with candles, matches, a bottle of holy water, and some bug spray. We are as ready as ever we shall be.

We arrive at our destination through a thin lake, happily riding in a pretty little boat, a pirogue. There is some painting on it, reminiscent of the Virgin Mary in the bathtub. The small outboard motor is less disruptive than the propeller boats that fly past us like waterborne aircraft. We troll near the edge of the lake to avoid the bigger boats. Most of us haven't been in this part of the world, in this sort of biosphere, and we find it very strange indeed.

Long tangles of Spanish moss dress the trees and wave gently in the breeze we make as we go by. Occasionally, a fat black snake swims beside us for a while, and we watch its shining black eye as it swims with the same motions that move it across the land. As we approach the farthest end of the lake, our boat takes a sharp turn down a little canal and the sky above us is mostly blotted out. It is then we notice the weight of water in the air around us. We have lost the cooling breeze of the lake, and we instantly feel the shift in the atmosphere.

A swamp is a peculiar place, not water and not land but both. Our boat moves through the middle of the channel, avoiding either side of the creek. Our navigator tells us that there is a "pretty safe" place up ahead a ways, a place where we can get out of the boat and eat our lunch. We question the idea of "pretty safe," and she laughs, calls us "cher," and gestures to tell us nothing is safe. We nod. We get it.

Throughout our travels, we have learned some big home truths, and one of them is that nowhere is really safe. There are places that are safer than others, places that hold a degree of safety that some—but not all—can access. We carry what safety we have with us to the best of our ability. Most of us come out of a dominant culture that constantly reminds us that we are not enough and that our safety probably depends on our value in a culture that consistently undervalues us.

At firesides, we have shared food and talk. The talk that happens after the easy tales and gossip—the talk that happens as the fire burns low and the night has set in always turns to the pain and the fury it sparks. We share stories of being physically, emotionally, and spiritually abused, and we go into detail, ripping off a scab and opening a wound that is gangrenous, debilitating. Wounds we have carried for so long now that we barely notice how they affect us, how they hamper us, how they were inflicted by other wounded people whose only relief from pain was to hurt others.

Maybe it's easier to feel anger and hate because we see that modeled for us all the time, in social media, in film, in our relationships. But that is a trap, too, because too often the person who inflicted the wound is someone we opened our hearts to—a mother or father, a lover, a trusted colleague. That open heart-wound bears the marks of strong trust betrayed, of love twisted into something no longer recognizable as love. The wound never heals properly because we haven't addressed that love/abuse cycle in any healthy or direct way. So we mash some antibiotic ointment into it, we strap it up, we learn to exist with it, we forget about it.

We have sat around that low fire, talking and weeping, until the sun began its rising.

The creek sides are closing in on us, and our navigator is slowing down to show us the cypress knees that are all around us. Almost everything here feels foreign but beautiful. The moss on the trees, the croaking frogs, the birdsong of birds we don't see. But these pale rounded lumps protruding from the water, so close that we can reach out and touch them, are mysterious and intriguing.

Our guide tells us that cypress knees grow up from the underwater roots of some cypress trees and can be found on dry land, too, around the base of the trees. There are theories about what they do for the tree and the environment but there's no agreement. People harvest them for craft projects, but she thinks they should be left alone. Cypress trees grow slowly and live a long time—would any of us want to live out our long lives with some of our parts missing? She shakes her head. Besides, there's spirits in the knees. Sometimes good ones, sometimes nasty ones. We want to hear more about that, but we have arrived at our destination. The two sides of the creek bank have come together in a point, and a ragged wooden dock juts out into the creek. We pull to the side, and our friend powers down the motor and throws a loop of rope over the post at the end. She waits for us to get our gear and walk to the land end of the dock. She pops the loop off the post and tells us cheerily that she's going to do some fishing and will be back in about an hour. She winks as she tells us she won't be far away and will hear us if we yell.

Not very comforting but blessedly accurate. We watch her putter-putter away, waving.

There is a narrow path quite visible, and we take that rather than bushwhack our way through the dense underbrush. Staying on the path is potentially the best way to avoid snakes or to at least see them with enough time to avoid them.

It is the weight of the wet air that we notice first. We had a hot breath of a breeze when we were on the pirogue, and it was less in the canal than out on the open lake. Here there is no breeze at all, and the air is heavy. We glance at the Playmate cooler and resolve to wait until we get to our unknown destination before getting out that cool water.

As it turns out, we don't have long to wait. The path is a mostly straight line that ends abruptly in an open space where the sun is shining in. Our damp faces are met with a light breeze. We step into the clearing and notice that there is no way out except for the way we've come in, assuming that this place was not a natural occurrence but crafted by humans.

The second thing we notice is the bathtub grotto.

We gather around it just as we had done in our friends' yard. We marvel that someone hauled half a bathtub into the swamp and carried it to this place. We have been chasing the idea of wild worship, of a feral church where we can immerse our souls in profound connection with the oldest Power...and here it is! Right in the heart of the swamp.

Looking around, we see how lovingly tended this place is. To one side of the grotto, there is a low table with drips of candle wax and stubs of candles on it. The ground is cleared of sticks and leaves, as though it has been swept recently. We realize our friends must have come here ahead of us and tidied up for our visit.

Our gazes return to the grotto, and we throw a blanket on the ground in front of it, in front of Her. We begin to unpack our sandwiches and start with careful drinks of water. One of us pours a cool libation at the base of the statue, and we take a hard look at this swamp Mary. She is very different from the standard Blessed Virgin Mary and is even different from the one in the grotto in the yard.

She is completely unclothed, save for a light blue cloth scarf that someone has draped over one of Her shoulders. The snake has moved up onto Her arm, and its head is near Her left ear, as though it is whispering to Her. As in the other statue, this Mary is looking directly at us. But Her look is ecstatic, Her eyes wide as though an orgasm is very near. Her lips are slightly parted and curve up at the corners of Her mouth. And in Her right hand, She holds an apple, a red and bitten apple.

She isn't Mary at all. She is Eve. She is the despised Mother, on one hand accused like Pandora of bringing all ill to the perfect world. On the other hand, She is despised for being the one who stayed, who didn't flee like Her predecessor, Lilith, to have wild sex on the beach. Eve is one who demurred and was subjugated.

We sit down on the blanket and watch Her, not believing our eyes or our hearts. The candles in the satchel are brought out and set on the ground before Her, lit and pushed into the soil so they don't fall over.

We eat in silence, tasting the food we are eating, intentional about drawing nourishment into our bodies—nutrition that is also spicy and flavorful. Our mouths begin to water, and we sip more water. A sandwich is offered at the base of the grotto among the candles.

She seems so alive, so present, and we are the welcome voyeurs as She eats the apple. *See?* she seems to say. *Do you see what I've done? That tree of knowledge over there—I took this fruit from it, and it is luscious. I was told I shouldn't do it because then I'd gain all the knowledge ever known. I couldn't resist it—could you? To be fair, this snake warned me to protect me—because once you are aware, you can no longer be unaware. Once you know, you can't unknow. Knowledge is power, but knowledge in the wrong hands—in the witches' hands, in the heretics' hands—must be punished and diminished, accompanied by pain and exile. I was told as you are told that you are never enough to matter, can never measure up to an approved standard. You must be subdued and restrained. You must be owned by superior beings to keep you contained and to keep you safe. But here's the truth—you are enough. You are perfect. You can be free.*

The smile seems to broaden and the eyes to narrow. *That feels like love until it doesn't. It is never to keep you safe. The only safety they are concerned about is their own. We are the dangerous ones, the powerful ones. Our freedom terrifies them. We must be controlled and contained. But that isn't possible, is it? Without reducing us to nothingness, to invisibility, they can't be safe. Even if it kills us, even if the Divine and Birth-Filled Woman must be buried, destroyed and forgotten, forever.*

Don't forget. Remember Her, remember me. Speak our names.

Eat the apple. Share everything you eat of that tree of knowledge. Eat the apple.

We finish the sandwiches and eat the fruit, too. We carefully pack up our wax paper bags and drink a little more water. The blanket is shaken out and folded, the candles extinguished and put back into the satchel. The statue in the grotto has returned to itself, concrete yard art painted by an outsider artist to portray a strange swamp Mary who looks an awful lot like Eve.

We have been away in this sacred clearing for about an hour and know it is time to return. We are packed and ready to move on but can't seem to leave. It does feel safe here, in spite of the boars and gators and snakes. We have known all along that there is no one place that is the feral church of our visions, but this place is one of them. On some level we all know we'll never come back here, only hold the memory of the place and the teaching of the Despised Mother forever.

One of us moves forward and kneels to touch the bare feet of the swamp Mary, then leans forward to kiss Her cheek and adjust the scarf. She turns to join us, and we go back the way we had come, thoughtful and also watchful. We have on our sturdy boots and carry our inner safety with us, of course. But we are aware that the swamp is a place filled with life and death. As is every place on this blessed Earth.

You are enough. You are perfect. Eat that beautiful apple and reveal all that hangs on the tree of knowledge.

Our friend and her boat are waiting at the dock. We clamber aboard, stow our gear, and settle ourselves. She asks if we found the grotto, and we laugh together at the chapel in the swamp. Weird and beautiful, we agree. She has caught enough fish for frying tonight, and we head for home.

Eat the gumbo. Eat the apple.

Perceptions

When we deny ourselves simple pleasures, we are replaying old ways of being trapped and judged in the world. But not old enough. Many forms of religion are adamant about the followers abstaining from even the most basic pleasure. There are sects that don't allow dancing or music. Others insist on particular kinds of dress that constrict the wearer. Many religions frown on giddy, earthly pleasures because their roots are in the denial of the flesh and the exultation of the soul. Some sects are slowly dying, fading into history, because their adherents aren't allowed to have sex, not even for procreation.

We know of older ways, and our journey to the feral church is allowing us glimpses into other ways the world can be and other ways that communities once were. When we embrace pleasure and find joy in the act of living in such a place, we begin to set aside these restrictive notions of how we live rich lives and achieve knowledge and even wisdom.

Margaret's Gumbo

Margaret Dahm is a true daughter of the Gulf Coast, and her gumbo is deliciously typical. She and I offer it here to give you an authentic taste of the bayou to remind you of all we learned in our pilgrimage to the Despised Mother and Her descendant, Mother Mary.

Ingredients

⅛–¼ cup oil
1 cup plain flour
2 onions, chopped
3–5 cloves garlic, chopped

1 cup celery, chopped
1 cup diced peppers
1–2 cans diced tomatoes
1 pound frozen sliced okra
3 tablespoons Worcestershire sauce
Salt, pepper, and tabasco or cayenne to taste
Meat and stock (see page 122)

In a large cast-iron skillet, make a roux by heating the oil and flour, stirring constantly. Seriously, stir constantly or the flour will burn and be ruined, so stir like mad until it turns about the color of peanut butter. Remove from heat and toss in chopped onion, garlic, celery, and bell peppers. Stir and add enough water to cover.

Add the rest of the ingredients (except meat and stock) and simmer for quite a while. But not over such a hot burner that the gumbo sticks on the bottom. If it does stick, pour the gumbo into a new pot without scraping the old pot. Once it turns into a soup-like concoction, check your seasoning and add more of whatever you think it needs, but be careful about adding too much salt.

Pour a small cup, taste it, and then add a bit of whatever is needed, more heat, more spice. If it tastes better in the cup after your additions, then it's the right thing to add to the pot. If it starts tasting pretty good but is still too thick, add stock and then your meat. Simmer together.

If you're adding meat: Ham stock is incredibly rich (ham cubes in chicken stock less cloying). With fresh or frozen shrimp (peeled), stock can be made from the shells. If you add sausage, brown first and deglaze the pan to save that flavor. Poultry is easy. Gumbo z'herbes (des herbes) is great and traditional during Lent. It's just meatless gumbo with a lot of greens. The story is that the more different types of greens you add, the more friends you'll make that year.

Chapter 10
TEA AND WISDOM: THE BOOKSHOP OF THE ANCIENT MOTHERS

There are many ways to think of and to access the Akashic Records, that place that holds all the wisdom and dreams of the ages, past, present, and future. The name comes to us from Theosophy, and the concept of such a compendium can be found in many cultures. This Hall of Records is in a surprising place in my own homeland of Appalachia. We will see what we find in this marvelous place.

THE JOURNEY

Going down this steep mountain highway can be challenging in not knowing when and how often to apply the brakes. Not often enough and your car takes the wild curves at a disconcerting rate of speed. Applied too often or too firmly and the acrid reek of smoking brakes will follow you for many, many miles. Slow but steady braking before a curve and easing off as you come out of it—this time-tested braking technique has served many generations of mountain travelers very well.

We are watching for our exit, which is about halfway down the dangerous road. Bags of carrot sticks, peanut butter–smeared celery, and corn chips pass back and forth, and there is nervous chatter to accompany the crunching. There is a state highway sign to warn us of our upcoming exit and the brakes are tapped quite firmly three times. The highway exit is negotiated, and we circle around and onto another decent road that takes us north, heading again into the high country.

Here in the old mountains, there is a dearth of direct roads: it is rare to be able to drive as the crow flies. Our journey to this Hall of Records is no exception. An interstate highway leads to a good state road that leads to a rutted state road that leads to a county road that finishes on a gravel-topped dirt road. We have taken the correct exit from the first highway, but there are several twists and turns ahead of us, both literally and metaphorically.

This new road takes us sharply uphill, and we pass small businesses, churches, and strip malls. There are wide access roads to several gravel pits and signs warning us that large trucks could be entering the highway along those points. We ride on, untroubled by such warnings. Miles to go, the road curves this way and then back again, like the tail of a dragon. At last we are told to look for a sign that marks where we make our next turn. We see it at last and are onto a less rigorously maintained state road, one that again winds its way upward. Next is a turn to the right.

Tea and Wisdom: The Bookshop of the Ancient Mothers

The sign for it has been knocked over and is being smothered in honeysuckle vines. There are fewer buildings along here. It is mostly small clapboard houses and the occasional still-occupied tar-paper shack, all with sloping front yards adorned with concrete statues. Deer families are prominent, as well as garden gnomes. There are also trailers of varying vintages in a variety of conditions. Pastures hold cows, horses, a few mules, and, surprisingly, some curious llamas. Chickens sometimes strut in front of the car, and we wait as they cross the road.

The only businesses are old convenience stores whose dusty pumps no longer distribute gas. Neon ads for smokeless tobacco and beer brighten the front windows with reminding posters of lottery tickets that will change lives, if you win, which you surely will one day. If we went inside, we'd find plastic-wrapped pastries and hot dogs on a revolving spit, well-cooked. The young woman behind the counter would be sassy and friendly, and you would leave with an empty bladder and some good advice about men.

But we won't stop this time, as we are near our destination. We are on the lookout for a small strip mall, and it will be on the left. It's a business center with only three businesses—there is a surprisingly good Honduran restaurant, a nail salon, and, at the end farthest from the road, a bookshop.

We pass more houses and trailers and one old-fashioned church, small with a tall steeple and red doors that open toward the road. It is well-kept and looks freshly painted, a violent white against the green of the woods and the blue of the mountains. Its graveyard is large and the stones tilt every which way. It looks well and often used and cherished.

It is the last building we see before we round a curve and see the strip mall in front of us. It is exactly as it was described, but it seems the nail salon has gone out of business. There are a few pickup trucks at the Honduran restaurant, but its lighted sign says it is closing in about forty-five minutes. We pull our vehicle to the back and park it in front of the bookshop. When we get out, we can smell the food cooking at the restaurant and consider stopping in for a bit before going to the bookshop. *Baleadas* could be ordered to go, to eat later. We decide against it, our tummies making sad noises. We turn to our destination.

It is, from this vantage point, completely unremarkable, except for the doorway. It has the same cheap siding as thousands of these mini malls throughout America. There is a rusted portico that keeps some of the rain off before you go in the shop's door. The building looks as if it has withstood much harsh weather despite the cheapness of the construction and the poverty of its location.

But the door. That door is extraordinary. It is not the heavy glass door that is pushed as you enter and pulled as you exit. It is solid wood, cherry maybe, rich in texture and color. There is no window—we notice then that there are no windows at all at this end of the building. No display places for the best sellers, no jolly visual displays of children's books. Just those metal walls with their dents and abrasions. There is only a handwritten sign in a picture frame hung to the right of the door. It reads,

Book Shop
Used and New
Mostly Old

No opening hours or days, no phone number in case of emergencies. No saucy name, like Book Du Jour or Black Mountain Books and Gifts. Nothing. Below the sign, on the concrete ground, is a bone china cup and saucer. The cup is empty.

We stand in front of the door and wonder. Is it open? Do we knock? There is a brass handle—do we pull or push? The fact is we are confused and a little scared—to hesitate is to buy some time before we face this task. Some of us take others' hands and offer a quick squeeze. Some are taking lung-filling breaths. At last, one of us takes the handle firmly, pushes down on the lever, and pushes, hard.

Nothing happens. Again the firm, confident grip, and this time a pull. The door opens so quickly that we all step back. Then we laugh and peer into the dark interior.

There are three rounded steps that lead to a lower atrium. They are carpeted in thick dark green carpet and take us to another door. This one is a plain wooden door and looks old and well used, like the church we passed on our way. There is a small light hanging from the ceiling, a single bulb in a shade of wrought metal, but it gives us enough light to see our way. Stepping onto the steps, we feel the luxurious carpeting, so clean, so elegant. The door opens easily and we find ourselves in an impossibly large space.

The carpet continues here, and the feel of the place is that of a Victorian gentlemen's club. The air smells of books and black tea, with just a hint of cigar smoke and lavender. It is a warren of rooms, as we soon find, all as dimly lit as the atrium. But the feel of the place is quite warm and welcoming, even cozy. We find ourselves stepping out to explore what is around us, and within minutes each of us is alone, separated from the others, enchanted as we are drawn into this charming place.

It is utterly silent, no music, no muffled conversations, no clink of spoon against cup. The carpet and the drapes that line the walls are partially responsible. But there is magic here, old and civilized magic. We can feel it and we are drawn into it. The feather bed enchantment is almost complete.

As we will discover later, we each have a similar experience in this place of memory, this hall of the Wisdom of the Ancient Mothers. After a brief exploration, each one of us comes to an alcove with a chair and small table. The table is set for tea, with a cup and saucer, a cloth serviette, and a little silver spoon. There is a fat brown teapot with a flowery tea cozy wrapped around it, fragrant steam wisping from the spout. A plate of sandwiches and a plate of pastries are stacked on a serving stand. Sugar cubes tumble together in a bowl and a tiny pitcher of cream sits beside it.

Each of us sits, pours a cup of tea to our liking, and drinks. Each of us takes a sandwich from the plate and rests it on the saucer before eating it. Each of us dunks a shortbread cookie into the tea and sits back with a sigh. We were uncertain about this task, but we are completely certain about this old-fashioned comfort and hospitality. Each of us relaxes, and that is exactly how we must be to look at the ancient records of our lives, our ancestors, our interlocking histories, and the civilizations and cultures that have brought us here, to this impossible place.

Each of us wipes our mouth on the serviette provided and places it, folded, onto the table. We are ready to scoot the chair back and rise when we hear, at last, a sound.

We hear a humming so soft that we wonder if it is a trick of our ears. But as the sound grows louder, we understand that we are not alone after all. When the tiny stout woman comes around the edge of the velvet curtain, she is unsurprised to see us, for she has prepared this space and this experience for each of us and has awaited our coming for some time.

Sitting in that delicate chair, each of us freezes, rabbit like, to watch her. She smiles and nods her head. We do the same. She tells us she is the recordkeeper for the bookshop and explains what will happen next. She is very matter-of-fact, but her words have a chilling effect on each of us. She waves her hand in the direction we must go. We rise and walk past her, each of us alone as we approach.

It is surprise after surprise here, and we suspect it is designed in such a way to encourage us past fear and into curiosity and the thirst for the knowledge that the bookshop contains. So the counter that stretches before us is strange but perfectly in keeping with all we have seen and done thus far.

It is the gleaming wooden bar of a saloon, like the ones in Western movies. There is a bar-back with a painting of the bookshop, but there are no liquor bottles, no glasses, and no mirror. There is no mustachioed bartender or silk-draped madam. Once again, each of us is alone as we finally reach the records we have been seeking: the records of past, present, and the times to come. In this place, time is neither linear nor circular. It is a living and unpredictable river of history and wisdom, a place from which any tidbit of wisdom ever thought or ever to be thought has found its place in the stream of the Ancient Mothers.

Each of us steps to the bar, and as instructed, we lay our hands flat on the surface of the bar, palms down. In a moment, a large leather-bound book comes whizzing down the long expanse of the bar and lands at our waiting hands. The book one needs is always the first to arrive, and we open with alacrity and begin to read.

It isn't only reading, of course. There are videos that play in our heads, music that fills our hearts as we learn and listen. All come from the pages of this and every book in this sacred place. When one book has filled us, we close the cover, take our hands away, and break the connection. It flies back the way it came, and we take a breath and place our flat palms on the counter once again.

When the history or the knowledge is too much, too harsh, a serviette like the one on the tea table appears before us to hold the tears, to absorb the cries. When the delight overwhelms us and we laugh too long or sing a song from our grandmothers, a heavy glass of water appears at our elbows.

In this way, we individually pass the short hours until dawn, though we don't know it. To us it feels like a brief time to spend in so powerful and important a place. But when it is time for us to leave, the books no longer slide down to us, even if we pound our palms on the bar. The lights in the bar-back go out. The glass and serviette are withdrawn.

There is nothing for it but to turn and find our companions. Somehow we gather back at the simple door that leads to the atrium. We smile to see each other, alive and whole. But we are all bleary-eyed and hollow, for we have seen so much that we are speechless, living still in the enchantment of the records. We think we catch a glimpse of the Recordkeeper, wheeling a tea trolley, humming. But she may have been an illusion, a mirage.

We go out the door and the overhead light is out. The only illumination comes from a small lantern by the door, and we use its light to go up the steps and push open the cherrywood door. We blink like owls to discover that it is morning, and we have been reading our collective histories the whole night through. No other cars are in the parking lot, and the prep cooks at the Honduran restaurant haven't arrived yet.

The van is waiting and we get in, still silent. We will go only a little ways up the mountain now and crash for the rest of the day at a little motel near the ridge. Then we will talk. Then we will share. But not now. To have been in such a place at such a time—for now, that is enough.

Perceptions

It is glorious to imagine a place that contains all the lore, the emotions, the wisdom of the universe and all it contains, but its practical good is even more interesting to consider. Certainly, we should be able to access our personal deep selves and improve our souls in a more organized way than humans generally do.

If you can peel back the layers of personal history and the influences that have held you back, it is possible you can move forward with more confidence and even ease. But if our journey in life is to learn through experience, you might end up not having those experiences that will truly bring you wisdom.

Theosophy presented us with the Akashic Records, and yet the world continues to turn, war and famine continue to counter any work for peace, humans continue to behave in the most human of possible ways. Perhaps we should access that bookshop more often. Or perhaps we learn best through doing. Life is experiential, after all.

Chapter 11
BLOOD AND BONE

We stay in the old mountains of my home for the next leg of our journey and will meet another aspect of the Old Woman of Winter. She is not one who will bring tea and cakes. She is the Bringer of Death, the Beloved Crone.

THE JOURNEY

We think that the peculiar journey up the mountain and into the bookshop gave us little preparation for the next part of our sojourn. But as we duck under the straggly limbs of the trees at the woods' edge, we hope we have learned something to add to our pocketsful of bread crusts and wisdom.

The path beneath our feet isn't very path-like. It is packed earth with stones emerging at odd angles, perfect for stubbing a toe or sending someone headlong into the dirt. It isn't straight, nor is it curved in any recognizable pattern, but it wends its way through shrubs and weeds then stops abruptly at the base of a large tree.

If we peer around the side of the tree, hand resting on shaggy bark, we see the trail continue on the other side. Did the path exist before the tree grew, or did whoever or whatever created the path ignore the obvious blockage and begin again on the other side, without also leaving a path that circled round the old tree? We can consider that as we move on, for we have business far into these woods, and to wait on our curiosity is not an option.

There is a musty smell here on the other side of the tree. The tree limbs are lower than before, and the scraggly undergrowth that lines the way leans in on us, poking, scratching, preventing anything like speed of movement. So we slow down. We turn sideways. We hold arching thorned canes for the ones who come after us.

The smells have certainly changed. In addition to the mustiness there is a sense of overall dankness. Before the tree, we breathed deeply because the air was relatively fresh and greenly scented. Now there is the unmistakable scent of decaying things, and dead ones, too. Like our breathing, our steps are labored and our tempers short. A little wind stirs the air, brings a smell of fear, and is gone. Our own fear, no doubt, but who else is cringing in the half-light around this awful trail? We are impatient to leave the wood or at least to get to where we are going. There is a sharp cry from someone near the front of the group and we all stop, listening, anxious. *Are you okay?* The muffled voice replies, *Yeah, smashed my foot against a rock.*

Are you bleeding?

I don't think so, but maybe. I can't tell. But I'm okay.

Okay. Be careful. Someone laughs.

We start again, more slowly than before. The terrain is changing again, with glacier-shoved boulders crowding the path, replacing the scraggle of sticks and thorns. The boulders are somehow worse than the brambles. Heavy and implacable. There are new stones on the trail itself, loose ones that roll underfoot, as well as broken sticks from the canopy above.

It was the middle of the afternoon when we entered the wood, and it is daylight still, though we cannot tell. The heavy canopy blocks most of the light, leaving us in a watery greenish twilight.

We stop now, looking up like tourists at the Empire State Building. Birds are chittering up there, the first nonhuman sounds we've heard in a long, long time. We didn't miss it, to be honest. The path had been so challenging, occupying our bodies, and our worrisome encounter ahead had occupied our minds. We have not been so focused on the pleasant parts of where we are—only a kind of dread about the path ahead.

The birds aren't singing, they aren't marking territory. Different species speak sharply. One holds the floor for a moment, then another answers. Around and around, a council held high above our heads, away from our view. Away from us. For all the world it seems as though they are having a meeting, and we fancy it is about us. Perhaps we are too self-focused—after all, we have almost drowned, we have broiled in the desert, we have left the comfort of home and garden to find the Goddess in the world and in ourselves. This pilgrimage has been about the beings we need to encounter, must encounter, in order to weave ourselves into the holiness of the world and the Goddess, to bind ourselves once more into the wild of the world as it expresses itself in us, where it has been deeply buried for so long that its rot has created fresh new and desperate wildness within, a wildness that must find itself in the feral lands, the undiscovered country. And here we are listening in on a conversation not meant for our ears.

Standing very still, barely breathing, we take in the forest around us, without fear for the first time. These trees are not only large; they are old. We know this because of the breaches in their sides, where the bark has been damaged and bald patches show the living wood underneath. Broken branches are everywhere around us, and we recognize the broken stubs of formerly healthy limbs protruding from the wide trunks.

Below the canopy, the shrubs and wild vines have been starved of light, and they show the lack. In most places, plants would not choose to grow where they don't have their needs met. Not enough nutrients, sun, water—a wayward seed that germinates in the wrong place will perish before it can set its own seed and reproduce. But here they are, plentiful but miserable, scraggly vines leaning on terminally ill trees and others stretching out into the pathway to make it as impassable as they can.

When we turn our heads to search the way we have come, we can just make out the large boulders at our last rest stop. In this landscape they seem oddly placed, we realize for the first time. Where did they come from? There are no nearby alpine slopes for them to have slid down. Were they delivered by ancient glaciers and then the forest grew up around them?

Are they part of an old landscape, or are they the future of this dying woodland, the doom of trees?

Because we are suddenly attuned to our senses, we realize the birds have concluded their meeting. Raising our faces to the bit of visible sky, we see the birds are looking down on us, their heads turned so their bright eyes can focus. The woods are once more silent, and we find ourselves turning from the birds' stare to look at each other. One of us reaches out a hand. Another takes it and reaches out another. Soon each of us is holding the hand of another, and we wait, letting the knowledge of our whereabouts glide from one hand to another, one heart to another. We nod. We know.

These are the dying lands. We assumed they must be encountered at some point. Dread is not too strong a word for the feeling that sweeps over us now, as we stand hand-in-hand under the dying trees and observant birds.

We nod to each other and drop hands. A mockingbird begins its weird and stolen song and is joined by others of his kind. Not a symphony but rather a jangling round of copied calls. Next comes a blue jay, squalling like a cat in the trees. More jays respond. Songbirds are next, and the cacophony is almost unbearable. The cries grow louder and louder until we hear the high and piercing cry of a big hawk, far into the darkening sky. The other songs dim then, and a trio of crows finishes the dark concert with their guttural "going home" call.

All is silent once more and we move forward into the gathering gloom. Determined now, the lessons of this long sojourn are bright and immediate again. The dying lands will bring us to the chthonic Goddess who has set Herself at the center of the earth's experience. She has been called the Queen of the Below, the Goddess of the Underworld, the One Who Cuts the Cord of Life, Death-Bringer, Cailleach. We will soon learn Her name here.

We carry small lights with us and use them sparingly. Now they are necessary. We are aware of rustlings in the underbrush and things that scurry across our feet as we walk. None of those can scare us now. We speak to each other in quiet voices, no longer hesitant to break an eerie silence. We are eldritch once more, reveling in our feral selves, recalling the self that lives beneath culture and upbringing. Someone is laughing and we all join in. It is a cry of triumph as the path begins to rise before us. We are in the foothills now, following the decrepit woodland as it creeps up the flank of the hills. We laugh still as the rustling in the dying underbrush intensifies.

The canopy has thinned and much more of the night sky is observable. The Milky Way spins above us and the barest scraping of a Moon shyly rises. The trail has also smoothed, and the way ahead feels much easier than before. We are being pulled into an area ahead, energy pulling at us from in front and pushing us from behind. We are moving faster than we have in this woodland, and it is a little disconcerting. But it is the next challenge on our pilgrimage, and we are now anxious to begin.

The path is steeper but clearer, the underbrush and scant trees thinning quickly. We come to a ridge, nearly treeless, and we smell rank herbs burning. Our noses are keen and we recognize mugwort, catnip, and some pungent mint. As we look down into the narrow valley below, we see a great cloud of it rising from an iron washing pot that sits in the yard of a small house. The house is a wooden one with a porch on the front under a steeply pitched roof.

A bent figure pokes the wash pot, and more smoke billows up. The figure carefully returns to the porch, climbing the steps slowly, waving a hand to direct the smoke. Turning to sit in a chair, we see that it is an old woman, hooded and cloaked. Before She regains her seat, She has pulled back Her hood and unfastened the clasp at Her throat, letting the cloak fall onto the chair. She sits, grasping the handles on the chair and adjusts Her feet on the floor.

She turns Her head and looks at us.

We wait, wondering what the protocol for such an encounter might be. She is a Crone—the Crone of Crones—and not a person to insult. There is an uncomfortable moment, then She raises Her hand and gestures for us to approach. The way is clear and easily managed, but we approach slowly, considering who and what we are invited to encounter. We have traveled the dying lands and have come to this place of tangible power. The hairs on the backs of our necks and on our arms have risen as we step forward. Behind us, on the ridge, a trio of crows perches in the last raggedy tree and watches our descent.

We fan out as we approach, and our hands go to those clever pockets in which all necessities seem to lie. One has a faceted stone, another a sweet wrapped in bright paper. Each has something unique, a talisman that reflects something of the personality of the one who carries it.

The smell of the smoke lingers in the air as we approach the wash pot, though the smoke has died down now, drifting away on that east-seeking breeze. We stand at the base of the porch and wait for the next instruction. The porch has a small table on it, near the chair, and a large spinning wheel on the other side of the woman. The table holds a pair of scissors, a couple of shuttles, and a bowl that looks to have been made from a gourd. The bowl is full of pork bones. No water cup or plate of bread, for these are unnecessary in this place, for this being. As we watch, She takes up one of the bones and gnaws at it, finally extracts the marrow, and sucks it down. The old woman wipes Her mouth with the sleeve of Her dress and wipes Her hands down Her skirt.

She stirs in Her chair, rearranging the messy cloak. Her bony hand reaches out and spins the big wheel, and we notice that there is unspun wool pooled at the base of it. The spindle holds a substantial hank of spun yarn in a variegated set of colors. The yarn on the inside of the hank is bright but is shadowed by the more recent spinning, which is grayed out. The thickness has changed, too—the yarn underneath is thick, while the gray yarn on the top is considerably finer and less tightly spun.

We scrape our eyes away from the intense wheel and rest them on the old woman, who is gazing at us, one by one. There is a smile on Her face, but it is a secret sort of smile. There is not jollification in it, only a mild relief that Her work on this occasion will not be as onerous as it often was. She clears Her throat and spits a brown stream off the porch, missing us entirely. That feels like a good thing, but we know better than to relax yet. Her hooded eyes are fixed on us, and we dare not look away.

A bony finger points to the person nearest the porch steps. The old woman mutters under Her breath, barely audible. The chosen person goes up the steps and comes to stand at the little table beside the old woman. Each one of us bears a gift—a stone or coin or sprig of wild plant—and that is offered to the Crone. The gnarled hand gestures to the table and the offering is laid there. The old woman beckons the giver to come closer, to bend down, to listen. There is much whispering, then, and gesturing. The giver's face grows pale, then nods once, quickly, and turns to leave the porch. Another brown stream streaks out of the old woman's mouth and the long finger points again.

This activity continues until each person, each pilgrim, has offered a gift and been given advice. After each one, the stream of brown tobacco juice jets into the yard. One is asked to stir the pot of smoldering herbs, and another is asked to sweep the porch. One by one, we come to stand before the Crone, and after making an offering and hearing Her counsel, we return to gather in the yard in front of the porch.

The last of us ascends the steps, tripping near the top and falling. The Crone rises swiftly and raises the seeker up, dusting, fussing. Then the old woman returns to Her seat and waits. As before, there is the offering and the beckoning gesture. This time, the gesture includes the whole group of us, and the whispered conversation is almost audible. The final seeker turns to us as the stream of brown shoots forth, some drops of it staining the old woman's dress.

She says to tell you who She is, since we already know what She is. In this place, She is called Plumb-Killt Woman. She spins the life of each of us, one by one, and cuts the thread when we are at the end of living. We have been respectful, as we should have been, and we have cheered Her. We are to take Her wisdom with us as we go, and we are warned not to forget what She has said, nor share it until we must. The seeker turns to the old Goddess. She nods Her head and rises up to put on Her cloak. Our companion joins us on the ground as the Crone, the death Goddess of this place, our Plumb-Killt Woman, opens the screened door and steps into Her little house. She turns and gestures to a rotting archway blocked by a small gate. Beyond it is a deeply rutted road that runs from Her yard and off toward the horizon. The Moon offers us little light to see how far it runs, but we gather near the archway to consider what we do next. The screened door slams shut, and we take out our little lights.

We don't know it but we are standing on an old corpse road. Throughout the landscape, these archaic roads are fading into the earth, but this one is sharp and very clear. We touch the wood on the archway as the gate creaks open. Behind us we hear peculiar music—from a stringed instrument, maybe—and it floats out on the evening breeze, replacing the smoke and the smell of mugwort. We pause, waiting. A voice as creaky as the door commences to sing a song, the words barely discernible.

> *Plumb Killt Woman stops Her spinning*
> *She closes her eyes for a rest*
> *Then back forward, back to front,*
> *She starts it all again.*
>
> *She's listening for that whisper.*
> *It is Her only job.*
> *To cut the dead from the living*
> *And sing the ending song.*

As we watch, the screened door opens and a stream of tobacco juice shoots across the porch and onto the yard. The door slams again as we turn to go through the gateway, ducking under the arch, and step onto the old corpse road, our little lamps doing their best to light the way from this dying land and into the west.

Perceptions

Mountain roads and pathways are often tricky and occasionally dangerous. Our journey to find out who we are and how we fit into a notion of a feral church has brought us twists and turns and surprising places that seem carved from dark wood, like Black Forest clocks. When the tiny door flings itself open, we have watched an insistent cuckoo either guide or chide us to continue our work. When we are confronted with that most ancient of blessings, Death, our desire is to paint Her with a beautiful and peaceful face. Needing to know what we can expect when Death comes is a fool's game. It is always best to greet the end of life as we lived the part that came before—with joy and adventure, regardless of the writings in the old Hall of Wisdom of the Ancient Mothers. Love every morsel of it that you can, and share those morsels as you are willing and able. That mean old spirit woman is waiting on Her porch for all of us. Every one of us.

Chapter 12
Dancing on the Corpse Road

When someone dies, they are given the respect due their station, the body tended and prepared. A box may be created to receive the physical remains, or the remains may be burned to ash or disposed of in one of many ways. A person of great standing will have a long line of mourners and a stone marker to signify their importance, even in death. Lesser persons will receive a less spectacular farewell. Such is the way of most cultures in the world.

The next part of our sojourn takes us to such a place, a final resting place. Legend tells us that the dead sometimes do not rest in these places but wander about, wraithlike. We are called to this hilltop to see the actions of grief and loss and to witness the ceremonies of death.

The Journey

The wind is sharp and biting, and we pull our caps over our ears and huddle together as we wait. The trees at the crest of the hill are old, as old as the stones that shelter under their canopy. They are oaks mostly, but mountain ash stands there, too, with a scraggly, bent apple tree planted there, facing the south. It is covered in pinkish blossoms made pinker by the light of the setting sun.

The oak is still holding on to some of last year's dried leaves, sucking every last sip of goodness as this year's buds emerge. The ash has new leaves, and the apple is sporting tiny leaves near the blossoms. Spring has been late here this year, and we were hoping for some soft weather after our time with Plumb-Killt Woman in her dank forest, a little respite to clear our heads of the repeated dying process we studied with that Gray Mamaw.

But it was not to be. The speed of our journey is increasing even as the intensity of the lessons bears down hard. The Darkening time seemed slow at first, and we could still recall the divine beings of summer and of spring whose lessons astonished us, left us gasping at the stab wounds that have accrued as our sojourn continues.

Instead, we are shifting from foot to foot, shivering in this vicious wind, and waiting. From this vantage point, we can see a rutted road that has been the way to this old boneyard since time immemorial. It is one of the old coffin roads that crisscross many country landscapes. Corpse roads, they are sometimes called. They were and are used to take the deceased from the place where they were eulogized to a church-approved burying ground. It is the next length of the road that brought us here from the dying lands.

It runs, like the "ribbon of moonlight" in Noyes's poem, straight as an arrow in the direction of the steeple on the eastern horizon.[2] From the lych-gate of the ruinous church, the dead were taken into the west, to the Land of Youth and the Apple Lands of the old Pagan folk. With the sun setting behind us, the road is barely visible, a ghost of itself, as it spools out into the distance.

There are stories of the places humans go when they die. Most of us were raised on two places—a paradise of everlasting bliss and an inferno of everlasting punishment, heaven and hell. The various religions know the rules that must be followed in order to achieve the former as well as the rules that, if broken, condemn us to the latter.

For the folks in this land, however, there was a different option. Upon death, the body of the beloved is washed, dressed, and dabbed with scented oils. She is dressed in a clean winding cloth and will rest on a table for the mourners to touch, to kiss, to grieve. When the approved time is over—and it ends more quickly in the hot summer months than in the preserving coolness of winter and early spring—the body is put on a bier to be transported to the west.

Sometimes a simple wooden box has been constructed for the journey. But more often the body is laid upon the bier and

---

2. Alfred Noyes, "The Highwayman," *Blackwood's Magazine*, August 1906, 246, https://archive.org/details/blackwoodsmagazi180edinuoft/page/n7/mode/2up.

is carried by family members and other mourners. The winding cloth is tucked in carefully against the wind and weather (and the jostling of the bearers) and is covered in branches of yew and masses of whatever flowers ornament the meadows and creek sides.

The way through the lych-gate is solemn and slow, but the road is daunting and soon there are songs to honor the dead and to discourage the spirit of the deceased (and the spirits of the road, too). Along the way there may be stories and prayers, especially at the coffin stones, where the bearers may trade places with walkers or merely rest for a moment before continuing.

This journey is best undertaken in late morning or early afternoon, for there are fewer wandering spirits about. It is certainly best for the burial to take place with the day at its fullest so that the mourners may return to that faraway steeple in a dignified way, solemnly and not at a trot.

There is no telling what has delayed them today, but we can barely glimpse some lights in the distance, lanterns carried for the return as well as the burial. It is a welcome sight.

We remain in our huddle but are also aware that we have been joined by some others, invisible others. That seems unremarkable in this haunted place, peopled with memories and history. The sun set some time ago and the shadows are dense. The invisible others don't jostle or threaten us: in fact, they seem blissfully unaware of us. They can be felt but not seen, and we are grateful for that simple blessing, as we focus on the lights that slowly move closer on the old corpse road.

The lights not only guide them on their way but also illuminate the walkers. We squint and seem to make out a dozen or more—some are carrying the wooden box, but most are surrounding the box on its journey, and a few stragglers trail behind it. All are dressed in appropriate funereal garb, and most have their bent heads covered.

One person is far ahead of the entourage and stepping livelier than the rest. Arms bent at the elbows, we are curious about this outlier until we catch the faintest of sounds. It is a fiddler, and the tune is not a dirge at all, not a murder ballad of the old times. It is a dance tune, brisk, spry.

Impossible, we think. Why would such a mournful group be led by such a one, with such an air? The lilting tune has no effect on the bulk of the party, their steps slow, evenly paced. It is quite a spectacle, and we forget our impatience and the biting wind as we wonder at the site. But the invisible others seem somehow livelier than before, and we imagine that they are slowly forming into recognizable shapes. We stand between these two phenomena and wait, our curiosity overcoming boredom and fear.

Closer and closer still until the fiddler appears over a hillock that marks a flattened place on the windy hill. There are black ribbons that stream from his elbows, and his clothing is tattered and worn. He stops his dancing and continues to play, his tune slowing a bit but never losing its fire. He looks neither uphill nor down but focuses on the bow and the fiddle.

The rest of the party tops that low rise and assembles around an old coffin stone, the resting place for the box before it reaches its final destination. The bearers set it down, and we can see it now. This wood box is as battered as the fiddler's clothing and has been used countless times along this road and others of its kind. It has taken many a shrouded corpse to the hole that awaits it, on this hilltop and others, both near and far.

The walkers put their lanterns on the ground around the box and step away, lining themselves up on the flattest part of the ground. They throw off their veils and cloaks to reveal clothing as worn as the fiddler's. The music stops then, and the fiddler watches the two lines that have now come to face each other.

We all wait. Time stretches like taffy; snapping back seems inevitable. At last the gathered dancers begin to clap their hands, a strong beat. The fiddler nods and bends to his work.

The dancers glide toward each other and clap the hands of the person opposite, then glide back to their own line. Forward and back, a loud clap the punctuation. The fiddler's tune is a jig now, though he doesn't dance. The walkers have become dancers, and their movements are mesmerizing, hypnotic. They turn and trot, preening and strutting, but their hands seem always to find the hands of their neighbors with a clap as sharp as gunfire.

We no longer mark our almost-visible others and step nearer the dancers. The old gravestones lean this way and that way, and we stop at last near the ones farthest from the trees on the hilltop. We can't help ourselves—we are drawn forward. The fiddler turns his face to us and motions toward us with his head. The dancers don't miss a step or a beat as they draw us into their strange twirling and clapping.

We are eager students and soon master the steps, even as the fiddler speeds up the tempo. We replace the dancers and are whirling on our own as the dancers become walkers again.

They don their coats and go to take up the box. As before, four carry it up on their shoulders and the rest walk behind. Up the hill they go, though there is no freshly dug grave in which to place the corpse.

The fiddler stays with us, though his head has turned and he is facing the entourage as it comes to rest under the oaks and rowans. We are dancing still, almost delirious with the speed and the joy of our bodies moving through space. We do not notice the box being set down. We do not notice that the four who bore the box all this way have taken out small tools and begin to pry the lid away.

The fiddler has slowed the frantic pace, and we are grateful to slow our own. Our clapping is not so sharp as it was in the beginning, and our feet begin to drag on the uneven ground. Our brains begin to clear, and we are blinking and shaking our heads as we come back to form two lines to face each other.

Two things happen then. The first is that the fiddler stops abruptly, the bow screeching across the strings. The second is that the lid is completely off the box, and from inside it emits a sound we have never heard before. A high cry of loss and grief, a lamentation of such weight that we turn to face the hilltop, dumbfounded.

The sound goes on and on, varying in pitch but never in intensity. The walkers bend over the box and help a figure rise from it, settling Her on the ground, holding Her arms as She continues the sound that has wound across the hilltop, through the leaning stones and into the softest parts of us. It is oddly soothing and terrifying, and though we have never heard it, we realize what it is. The woman has pulled back Her hood and

Her red hair flows around Her face. The sound She is making—the keening—is effortless to Her, something She has done since time out of mind.

Two of the walkers come to stand beside Her. One is a young girl, the other an older woman. They join in the keening, the old one bringing the lower notes and the girl weaving Her high voice into the lament. Something like words is being formed now, but it isn't in any language we know and is more word-like than actual words. We can hear "no" and "wo-wo-wo," and a line ends in the pitch rising in a soft grunt—"uh."

On and on it goes and we climb the hill to stand near them. The fiddler has caught something like a tune and joins the keening women with an air so plaintive that tears come sharp to our eyes. The melancholy is tangible. The walkers put the lid on the box and pick it up once more, turning to face the old corpse road and the way home. The fiddler's tune comes to a quiet ending, and he joins the entourage as it turns down the hill.

The three women continue Their toning and keening for a while longer, and we watch Their sad faces, realizing at last that They are the same woman. One in Her youth, one in Her age, one at the middle point of Her long life. As with the keening, we know who She is, who They are. Too often the Bright Arrow, Brigid of the Gaels, is seen as a gentle country woman, a clever nun, a generous beer- and bread-maker.

This is not that Goddess. This is the Brigid who brought keening to the people, who is also the Queen of the Dead, a Death Midwife of authority and power. The three women wrap

Their arms about each other and move as one to follow the walkers, to follow the little lights onto the straight road. Their voices float up to us, fading as the three become one. We watch Her small figure move along the road and disappear into the distance, alone, bereaved.

We sit now on the cold ground, drink some water, share some bread and dried fruit. We are frankly stunned by what we've experienced and also confused about what we should do next, where we should go next. Throughout our sojourn, we have always come to the end of one place and usually find the well-marked path to the next. We talk quietly about our dilemma. The decision is made to follow the walkers, fiddler, box, and Goddess along the straight track and see where we end up.

Rising, we dust ourselves off and stretch our arms and legs. The dancing has left us all a little stiff. We go down to the flat area and start over the brown of the hillock. We are tired and would like to sleep. But not yet, and not here. The hill path winds its way down to the straight-as-an-arrow road and the leaves crunch under our feet. We are glad to leave this strange place behind us and are still puzzling about the meaning of it all when we realize that the almost-visible ones are following along behind us.

We had forgotten all about them and are surprised to see them following, assuming that the hilltop graveyard was their homeplace and that they required little interaction from us. It seems though that the keening and dancing have sparked some energy in them. We sigh and accept their company, as though we had any choice in the matter.

We have taken out our own lanterns and the almost-visible ones seem to exude a faint shimmer, just like ghosts in films. The walkers are far away from us, so far that we can't see or hear them. So far that they might never have been. We don't talk much, whether from weariness or reflection. The first of the coffin-resting stones is ahead, setting halfway between the road and the verge. Our companions surge ahead of us and claim the stone. We stand around them, waiting.

Sit, says the one standing in the center of the stone. Surprised to be addressed, we sit. *We have been charged,* says the spirit, *to remind you of your place in the world.*

We bristle a bit at this. The point of this mad escape is to unsettle our place in the world, to run free, to find a place of wild worship of the wild Divine.

When you meet us, you meet beings who are part of the world and yet not part. We have been like you, living, mating, laboring. And then death came to abide with us, and we are in that world, too. Straddling both places, here and not here. But you are of the world still. Your spirits reside within frail bodies. Your spirits can be beaten down by circumstances, by your lack of will, by your weakness of body and mind.

You will leave this road now and take that path to the village. The house is there, the table set. We are jealous of your soon feasting, for that is lost to us.

We remember it. We remember fear and hunger and pain. We have felt grief and fury but no more. We envy you the terrors of flesh. We tell you now that these terrors, this anguish, and agony are what life is. To find the joy, to live life in the midst of all that is to live a life of meaning.

Do not delay. Live now, live in shadow and in the holy light of summer. Live in grief and love, in desire and in heartbreak. Too soon you will be as we are, in these pallid lands of nothingness.

Life is all. Ecstasy is all.

The speech is finished, and our companions are almost invisible again. We watch them flow back in the direction we have come, silent, no longer shimmering. How sad we feel, and how humbled.

The path to the village leads us away and we turn to follow it.

PERCEPTIONS

It is easy to mouth the platitude that death is part of life when you are not grieving or when your bereavement is not fresh. It is harder to be philosophical when the dying is fresh and hard. In much of Western culture, death has become something that is jobbed out to professionals. Lately, though, the work of midwives has extended to the end-of-life guidance for the dying and those who love and support them in the process. As we welcome a more human and hands-on approach to these processes, we find ourselves less frightened and far less intimidated by the idea of death. If we are fortunate to age, each passing year brings us more reminders of our own mortality as we come to terms with the mortality of those we love, our colleagues, our elders. Death is certainly one of the milestones in human existence, and making a good death is now something people actively discuss and plan. A good death varies depending on the one doing the dying, but it usually means being surrounded by loved ones, being confident about those end-of-life details, and not being in excruciating pain. Those are worthy goals when there is time to follow our death process. Sometimes death comes swiftly, without warning, and sometimes we can't manage the way the process runs. It is worth considering what you consider a good death and making some notes—or even preparations—for those powerful processes.

Chapter 13
Sin-Eating and Benedictions

Many of the cultures we inhabit encourage us to think of ourselves as spirits attached to a flesh suit we'll eventually part from. The body will be destroyed by fire or rot, but the spirit is the true self and is eternal.

This idea encourages us to disregard our physical selves, to allow our bodies to be used in unhealthy ways and to endure whatever comes in life, because after death we will go to a wonderful place. Not this precious Earth, where things are difficult, dirty, and painful. Let's spend some time in the city now and feel the embodiment of the flesh and the braiding of spirit and matter in the person of our exquisite selves.

The Journey

It is sundown in the city, and it is raining, the sort of rain that is steady, unrelenting. The city never stops for weather, so taxis crawl by the buses taking commuters home from work. The people are moving fast on the sidewalks, avoiding touching each other, avoiding tapping umbrellas. Tired children are dragged by the hand as they beg for a candy bar or escape their bondage to press a wet face onto a pet store window.

The streetlights are on, and the traffic lights are brighter than in daytime. Traffic is loud with horns and sirens, and the talk among walkers is loud to compensate. Everything is moving fast. Everything but us. We know where we're going, but we are early for our meeting and stand, dripping, under the awning of a store that is *Out of Business*. Phones and watches are checked for time and for messages and at last we move out onto a sidewalk less packed than it was just fifteen minutes before.

The rain is as strong as ever, so our collars get pulled up and umbrellas are lowered around our ears. We move together like a flock of gawky waterbirds, our destination a few blocks away.

After our travels in the natural wild places of the world, the city feels stranger than either woodland or prairie. We are missing the connections we made in the wild places and are on our way to meet a sin-eater, hoping for a way through the noise and busyness of the city. It is a way, we are told, that goes through our gullets and then out, creating compost, freeing us from burdens of shame and guilt, burdens that we have carried through our personal histories. The overculture inflicts its mores and standards on us, no matter how hard we try to avoid the contagion. So we carry it mile after mile, and it weighs us down like bricks in our coat pockets.

Sin-eating is a centuries-old tradition. No one knows where or when it started, and no one knows if the practice continues in secret places, like snake-handling. Class is wrapped up in the practice, as it is wrapped up in so much of the cultures we inhabit. If a member of a wealthy family died suddenly and was unshriven, a peasant was called in to "eat the sins" of the dead. We understand some villages had a particular person who took on the role and would be called in in the event of a sudden death. Most often they were men and received some coins in payment for the deed. He would then drink a tankard of ale and eat a loaf or cake that had lain on the chest of the deceased. Sometimes the cake was salted or had lain in a bowl of salt on the chest of the dead.

The practice was not widespread but certainly gets a grip on the imagination. It is the stuff of ghost tales and nightmares, and it must have been a sad thing to be the sin-eater for a community. That sort of healing and magic is a powerful gift, not lightly given nor deeply understood.

This new sin-eater is a woman, and she is reviving the tradition with intention and simple ceremony. She does not have a website or social media presence, and we understand she comes from a family of sin-eaters—a historic nugget she discovered while doing genealogy on a couple of sites. Her name is Flora, and it is a chosen name. She took the name of the wife of the last sin-eater in her family. She wrote a small paper for an obscure genealogy magazine, and that is how we found her.

Settling in the noise of the city felt right to her as the flow of energy took away some of the burden of her practice.

Her street is a small one but well-marked, and we find it even in the rain. Three steps rise to a stoop outside her apartment. A concrete planter full of petunias, soggy in the downpour, graces one edge of the stoop. There is a yellow light beside the door—she is expecting us. We press the buzzer.

The door opens at once and Flora stands in the spill from the yellow light, which gives her face a jaundiced sallow look. But she is smiling and welcoming, showing us into her mudroom, where we remove coats and stow umbrellas. When we are ready, she brings us into a large and plain room. There are chairs all around the edges, those old-fashioned bentwood chairs that were once so popular in pizza parlors. In the center of the room is a long dining table, scratched in places and completely bare. The tall narrow windows are hung with thick curtains so that no light gets in or goes out.

She invites us to be seated and we do, clustered together on one side of the room. She smiles at that and says that is often the way when people come for the ceremony. She's not sure if they are shy or frightened, but it doesn't really matter which one. They find comfort, as we are doing, in the closeness of the familiar, in the warmth of friends and family. Flora tells us the story of how she found out about what she calls "the family business" and how she decided to revive it for modern seekers. She bows her head to recall how she was bent over her laptop one night, making notes on her family tree, when she heard a voice in the other room. She put the computer on her desk and went into her small sitting room/kitchen and saw a woman standing at her kitchen sink. It was no one she knew. She didn't have a housemate or partner, and no one else had a key to her brownstone—she had made a point of having the locks changed a few years back.

The woman didn't turn toward her as she cleared her throat and murmured a hesitant "Hello?" Her clothes fit her very well and looked expensive, to Flora's eyes, and stylish. The phantom woman poured herself a glass of wine and stood there, still with her back facing Flora, the glass raised to her mouth. She drained the glass in one drink, then raised her hand to her mouth as she turned. Her face was pale as milk and her eyes sunken and dark. Prominent cheekbones and a high, wide forehead gave her face a cadaverous look, which startled Flora into silence.

I am not here to take you, she said, *but to teach you. I am She who transports souls to the gateway. I have many names in many places, for death is here for all. If you have a need to address me, you call me Momma.*

The strange Goddess stayed with Flora all night and guided her ancestor search as far as was necessary. Momma drank all the wine in the house and pointed with a long bony finger to the furniture layout of the large room. After hours of instruction in the ceremony and introduction to the ancestors that could be called on in time of need, Flora fell asleep, her head on her arms. When she woke, the coffee maker had been run and the smell was wonderful. Momma had left some instructions scrawled on a piece of paper from the recycling bin. Flora never saw Her again.

The original ceremony was simple. A flat bowl of salt was pressed onto the bosom of the deceased and scone-like cakes were set on the salt. A few coins exchanged hands and the sin-eater spoke a few words to transfer the sins from the soul of the deceased into the cakes and from there to the sin-eater's soul. The salt was there for purification so that no dribbling sins would remain.

Sometimes the family stayed to make sure the ceremony and the deed were completed properly, but often they left the room, superstitious that the transferring sins might somehow spill over onto them.

Silly, really, but it was a way for a poor person to make a little money. A savvy sin-eater would privately visit the local priest the very next day and have his soul cleaned through a flurry of Hail Marys and the liberal sprinkling of holy water. The village sin-eater, maybe, but not the village idiot.

Flora has been doing this now for six years. The funeral home brings the body into her brownstone and lays it on the table. They wait outside near the hearse, and she comes to the stoop when the ceremony is finished, signaling to them to bring the gurney up. The payment is considerably more than her ancestors made, and she has no issue with that. Her price is quite fair considering the uniqueness of the practice, and the city is an expensive place to live.

She is also working with a couple of psychologists whose practice includes patients with food issues and body dysmorphia. They refer patients to her when the doctors find the hidden reasons—the trauma, the abuse—for the patient's unease. Those patients come to stretch out on the table—under their own steam—and Flora performs the ceremony to relieve them of the hurt that they have been unable to heal. The bulk of her practice is this "sin" eating, and she weeps to see the hurt and the agony of the people who stretch out on her table, a small pillow under the head.

The ceremony is the same for both, but Flora finds that the work with her living clients is the hardest. To live in a culture that hounds people into an unachievable quest for physical perfection locks so many good people in an endless cycle of guilt, recrimination, and shame. Her ceremony often helps, and she sees sad and broken people leave her house with a lighter step and a smile. She doesn't charge for this work, but grateful clients send her letters full of kisses and cash.

Flora looks at each of us in turn, and we nod or smile back at her. But one pilgrim has scooted her chair to one side. Throughout Flora's account of her work, this seeker turned her head away or bowed it low. Now she is crying quietly and Flora steps toward her.

Child, have you been sinned against? she asks. The weeping pilgrim cries harder, and the person next to her reaches out with a wad of tissues.

Come lie on the table.

Flora leaves the room as we help our friend onto the table. She has stopped crying and is blowing her nose. She is covered with a wide scarf and another is placed under her head. Flora reenters with a bowl of salt. She invites us to circle round the table and she places the bowl on our companion's belly.

In the way of Spiritualist table-tilting, we are told to place our fingertips lightly on the edge of the table. Flora begins to speak, softly, slowly.

Sweet child, I am here for you. Your friends are here for you. You have come to this house of healing of your own accord, and here is the place of your deliverance.

Flora reaches out to touch the salt, her fingers plunging into the bowl.

Here is the tool to bring out that which has corrupted, that which has doomed you in this life. Here in the grains of this salt, I swear to you a solemn oath to remove the sins that were sinned against your body, your soul, and your heart. As I move the salt over you, let the wickedness that has confounded you and stifled you be lifted out of you and into this precious bowl.

Flora moves the bowl up and down over the still form. She passes it to the person nearest her and each of us in turn holds the bowl over our companion. There is an electricity that runs up from the floor and down from the ceiling, moving into our hands as the bowl is passed from pilgrim to pilgrim and over the silent body.

Flora begins to sing an unfamiliar tune and speak words at each break in the melody. We take up the tune, and in this way, the bowl is passed three times around the table. With each circuit, the energy moves faster as it enters us and then passes between us, creating a web that includes each one and covers the person on the table.

When the bowl returns at last to Flora, she holds it close to her chest for a moment and then her arms stretch up into the air, the bowl resting on her flattened palms. The web of energy falls away from us then and we slump a little, tired in ways we haven't known before.

The weeping pilgrim is no longer weeping and sits up on the table, blinking her eyes and wrapping her arms across her chest. We help her off the table. We all sit for a moment, watching Flora pour the salt into a glass container and wipe down the bowl. Flora leaves us and is gone so long we wonder if we should leave without goodbyes. Finally, the door opens and she is with us again, smiling.

We thank Flora for her kindness and her wisdom and for sharing that strange experience. We wish her continuing success and joy in her work, gather up our companion and our gear, and say goodnight. Flora opens the door onto a cool night and a clear sky.

Perceptions

Our kind host has welcomed us into an old practice made new. She is a creator who has found her own niche, one that works for her skills and is a gift to her clients, a gift that those clients may not know they even need. Flora exemplifies the ability of a free soul to expand what they know with curiosity and to make meaning in a world that feels increasingly meaningless.

Our pathworkings open new ways of thinking, reacting, and processing to us. Success, in whatever way we choose to define it, depends on our curiosity and courage, and on resilience, too. We can find feral churches, those salons of the Primal and Wild Mothers, in so many places—in cities, suburbs, wastelands, gardens, deserts. We only have to seek them out. We know that now.

Chapter 14
WENCESLAS AND THE FIVE OF PENTACLES

Folklore is filled with stories of kindly rulers who do their best for their people, contrary to what history repeatedly tells us. We want to believe that powerful people, wealthy people, and celebrities are good at heart, and we are often bitterly disillusioned when we discover that not only do our idols have clay feet, but those feet are filthy with corruption and cruelty. It is better to dream that those appointed by some Holy Force to have dominion over us are somehow superior to the peasants who serve their every need. We want to believe that the rulers are put in such an exalted place through divine right. Our social media–driven world shows us again and again what the real lives of "royals" look like behind the pomp and circumstance, regardless of the sphere over which they hold sway—politics, sports, fashion, finance.

An old-fashioned Christmas carol called "Good King Wenceslas" relates the story of a king who sees a peasant struggling in the snow on St. Stephen's feast day. His heart is touched by the person gathering scraps of wood to heat his distant house, takes pity on him, and orders his page to bring food, drink, and firewood. They head out to the peasant's house in the snow, and the page—who is apparently carrying everything—complains of the cold. The king advises the boy to walk in the royal footsteps and all will be well. From the well-stocked palace of the king to a lowly peasant hut at the edge of the forest, beside a holy well they go. We aren't privy to the delivery of the opulent goods nor to the return home.

In the tarot deck designed by Pamela Colman Smith, the Five of Pentacles depicts two people standing in a snowy street with a bright stained-glass window behind them. It is the Good King Wenceslas card. The smaller of the two figures is on crutches and the other is thin and bent, barefooted in the drifting snow. One interpretation of this card is the dual nature most people carry with them. It can also be interpreted as a reminder to treat oneself well, to practice self-care. We are stepping into the world of that card for our next pathworking to consider the ways in which we judge ourselves and the others around us, and that will require a setting for what lies inside the backdrop on the card.

THE JOURNEY

We stand on the white edge of the card as we imagine the scene rising before us in three dimensions. When we are ready, we step from the staging point and into the world of Smith's card and Wenceslas's drear and winter world. We see two people ahead of us; one is bent and barefooted. Her companion has a crutch under each arm.

Behind the two sad figures is a golden stained-glass window. We are venturing into the room beyond the window, away from the snow, a place of comfort and warmth. There a feast is laid on, a fire is in the fireplace, and soft music is playing.

We now enter that grand room beyond the stained-glass window. The floors are polished wood, set in intricate parquet patterns. It has the subtle ripples that indicate decades of use, years of dancing feet and running children. Here and there a woven rug adorns the beautiful old floor, reflecting the painted flowers on the ceiling above.

The ceiling is very tall, as one would expect in such a fine room. It holds plaster swirls and painted scenes. Old-fashioned lighting fixtures hang at intervals from plaster medallions, and sconces line the walls, giving off a soft and forgiving light. The walls are a warm shade, the color of faded roses. All the windows are made with colored glass, and slender doors open onto a terrace filled with pots of fragrant herbs.

There is a heavy door at the opposite end of the room from those glass ones. It is simple and curiously unadorned. A small window set high on the door's face gives a narrow view to the world outside. It has a shutter over it, like an old-time speakeasy.

The smell of food draws our attention to the table. It is long but narrow and heavily laden with dishes and platters. The smell is a mingling of roasted meats, grilled and buttered vegetables, and fresh loaves warm from the oven. One end of the table holds sweets and the opposite end little canapes, finger foods. A similar drinks table sits at a right angle to the feast, and we spy fine wines and drafts of beer. The dominant smell is coffee, and even those who don't drink it appreciate its aroma.

We are completely alone in this grand setting. No one has greeted us or told us to leave. Still we are a little uncertain of our welcome, though we know this is the next piece of our pilgrimage puzzle. Our collective curiosity overcomes our discomfort, and we wander quietly around the splendid room, noting the appointments, our mouths beginning to water from the smell of all that food. We give in to our appetites and step toward the feast.

We want to taste everything on the long table and circle around, sampling all the things that draw our attention. Bites of succulent chicken, little tarts made of cheese and fruit, pink shrimps on curly skewers—all were tasted, some more than once. The dessert plates are on tiered stands. We stand around them in solemn groups, using our eyes to imagine the flavors of the iced pastries and the little cakes. Was that pink one strawberry, or might it be cherry? A brave soul eats one and declares it raspberry. Round and round we go, until our bellies are full, and we turn to the music that has accompanied our feasting.

Near the terrace doors, a musical ensemble is playing complicated, quiet music from days gone by. They are focused and very skilled. Their music fills the air as deliciously as do all the aromas from the food.

The room is quite large and heated by a fireplace along one wall, the wall opposite the colorful windows. The fire is low now, banked as the room is set for the evening's festivities. It is deep, though, and can accommodate a large fire with no problem at all and never a smudge on the surrounding walls.

Such a fine place! After our travels, this all seems the height of decadence, of the human need to overdo, to overindulge, and to suck up all available resources in the fear that none will be left when needed. Where does this fear dwell? Perhaps we bring it with us in the memory of war and famine, of a lack of basic needs that is stamped on a species that prizes war and conquest. In such a world, with such a culture of competition and destruction, no group is safe, no one culture can escape the inevitable turn of the wheel.

These extraordinary urban settings should make us proud of the achievements of our species. But all we can see are the lights that stay on all night long and the table of food that is much more than we can eat. It is all so beautiful and so terrible. Our wanderings have given us a different way of looking at abundance and at those who are not at this glorious table. We take what we need here and refill our water flasks. Then we go through the terrace doors and into the brightness of the city at night.

It is then we see a small crowd gathered just below the golden window. Their clothing is ragged, many of them have bare feet though the wind is stinging, and the snow has an icy crust. Their faces are turned down, but we see the red cheeks and noses. They have little outer clothing, certainly no warm coats, and we look at each other in confusion and shock. When we turn again to look at that other crowd, we see they have turned to face us, their heads held high, their gazes steady. It is only then we realize that through some trick of time and space, we are that ragtag group. We are warm and well-fed. We are cold, hungry, and alone.

We walk toward the little group, unsure of what we should do or can do. This is not our house. There is no host to guide us in the ways of this town or its cultures. Hospitality is the great foundation of our human interactions, but this bountiful house is not ours to share. We have nearly reached them, or rather us. Each face is familiar and, at this stage in our yearlong pathworking, each face is beloved. We are these people and they are us.

We pair up with the one who shares our own face, and we reach out a hand to that beloved stranger. We turn to walk back through the street to the terrace and its potted herbs, catching the scent of rosemary. There can be no question now. These beings are to share in our good fortune, in the hospitality of people we don't know, though it may cost us dearly. We step back inside the warmth and the sweet air, and the room is filled with people, filled with welcome and delight. Relieved, we turn to our new companions and find they have disappeared and only we are left. That is when the lesson sets itself out for our knowing. To welcome oneself into the goodness of the world is no small thing. It requires courage and self-love, it demands that we understand our own values in the world.

We are embraced by our charming hosts, and the night continues until dawn begins to break in the east. This extraordinary vision of where we have come and to where we may be going is another hint at this world we are building. A world where welcome is the law and generosity a given. This requires neither the right of kings nor an unbroken bloodline of wealth and privilege. It requires seeing and loving what is and understanding the greed that is born of fear and hunger. We are to welcome ourselves—and with us, all the Others—into the warmth of human companionship, a place where too few are welcomed fully.

PERCEPTIONS

We walk in places bright and dark. All these places allow us opportunities to make our lives different, our communities different, our families different. Different is not always better, and our sharp discernment is necessary when we throw off the shackles of Abraham and reach for the wildness in each leaf of this feral church. Throw sin aside! Never let that rancid superstition confuse your mind or trouble your heart. Know your personal standards and ethics, learn them well, but don't carve them into stone tablets. We all are learning wisdom and humility on this journey, and both will serve us in the reforming of the beauty of the world and the worth of the peoples in it. Guilt is not a thorn to trouble your soul or your mind. Pull it out if you find it there, and compost it to make new soil for the seeds of our new world. Shame is a heavy burden that has been set upon us by other hands—throw it out! Let your soul and your heart be clear as you tread the path to Goddess and Her sweet world. Let guilt and shame and the quaint notion of sin disappear from you like smoke in autumn. Welcome yourself home. Welcome yourself in.

Chapter 15
TERRA MATER, THE MOTHER WORLD

We are nearing the end of our time together, and everything seems to be moving faster. Stop now and take some deep breaths. These next few stages in the pilgrimage take a certain amount of courage and encourage us to strengthen our resilience, to look in the crevices for answers—and to expect the unexpected. We are stepping into another of those ancient-and-modern concepts and will explore the idea of societies that are governed not by conquer and warfare but by nurturing and caring. It's called Mother World—Terra Mater—and we are anxious to see how that differs from the power-over systems we have seen too often modeled for us, in history and in the world all around us today.

The Journey

It is midafternoon and the beach is filled with noise and color. It is one of those early summer days when the sun is strong but the water not yet warm. Children are racing into and then out of the water, shrieking with shock and joy. Some middle-aged men, lanky in their baggy shorts, are building kites under a big red umbrella. They've brought a plastic folding table and are very serious as they go about their work. The mothers wear sensible suits and keep the sunscreen and endless supply of juice boxes cold in a Styrofoam cooler. They also have beach umbrellas, shades that have been used season after season, carefully stored in the garage in the winter, wrapped in a black leaf-collecting bag.

The tide has not yet begun its inward flow, so the splashing children and amorous teens move far from dunes to enjoy the cold water. The mothers have their weary eyes on their charges, and the men emerge from the tent to trot down the beach until the kites catch a breeze and fly aloft.

The clouds that were slinking on the horizon have risen now, even as the sun begins setting. They have changed to a red-tinged gray, rising up to block the sun and the horizon. The swimmers and their minders pack quickly, looking over their shoulders and calling in their shrill voices for the children to come out of the water. Even the kite fliers decamp, reluctantly lowering their treasures and wrapping up the strings. Only one of them remains, stubbornly guiding his kite along the shore, a New Age Benjamin Franklin. The beach is nearly empty and the tide has begun coming in, when the dense clouds pause in their journey and jagged lightning strikes the sea.

The low rumbling starts then, the clouds anxious to move along and butting heads with the ones battering the shoreline. Whether it is the thunder, the slashing lightning, or the threat of rain that compels him, the lone kite man impatiently jerks his kite from the sky, dropping it neatly into the oncoming tide. He throws down the ball of string in his hand and leaves it there on the sand, abandoning his game to the sea. The thunder is loud now and directly overhead, and the lightning strikes are coming faster and faster. He runs toward the dune as the rain begins to pelt down, hoping against hope to arrive home dry and unscathed.

The sea and the beach mingle together in their old familiar way, no longer plagued by the ridiculous humans and their toys. It is a wild symphony of sound and light and the implacable tide. There is joy there, a wild glee that land and sea feel in their commingling. Rain flows down into salt water. The impatient clouds win out in the end, and the storm moves on along the coastline. The tide flows with its back-and-forth motion, and the beach is once again clear. The storm masked the setting sun, and now all is twilight here, the stars not quite out, the Moon not yet risen.

We have gathered far from the bustle of the beach-in-sun and have mercifully missed the rain, too. We've watched it from a cave-like place in a cove to the west of the strand, and night has come early for us. We sit around a low fire and talk quietly of the world that is coming, the world we are dreaming, the world we are creating from the dregs of an ancient world that we no longer remember.

We are dreaming of a Mother World, a Terra Mater, a place that is being birthed. So many places have called to our rambling feet these many months since we tore through that dense hedge, looking for the sort of divinity and freedom most of us couldn't even imagine. Now we have come into a new place with a vision of more connections and, frankly, more magic. Our sojourn has tested us, and it has also given us a clearer vision of what we want—what we need—not only to survive but to thrive. As with most things, we were clear from the beginning of all this about what we didn't want, what we were fleeing as fast as our bodies and spirits could carry us.

We were sick of hierarchy and of conflict. The continuous imposition of competition on every facet of life has led us to distrust much of the world around us and much of our own species. We are hungry for strong and resilient communities that can stretch to fit newcomers who are seeking to live in a way that is helpful and nourishing. Nurturing each other and ourselves is a skill we have grown into on this journey: we have learned to speak out when we are tired, in need of water or food. We no longer feel we must be stronger and harder-working than the rest of the group to prove our worth, our value. These paths have shown us other ways of being and of creating, and we bring our new knowledge to bear on all the systems we see collapsing around us. We talk of forest schools for the children where their education includes the soil and plants around them.

There is laughter when we remember the house in the city with the food-laden table, and we become serious as we talk of planting food and processing it, as we ponder its distribution so that no child is hungry, no one is hungry. We puzzle over how elders can be treated as their bodies age and where they will be most content and conclude that place of honor in the heart of the family and community must be supported with more than words. There is a generosity in our conversation, and we realize we are speaking of the oldest of sacred rites, that of hospitality. In exploring this tantalizing world we intend to make, we are dreaming strange visions of what family can look like when it is expanded to include several generations of love and tending. Our quiet voices rise in excitement, then fall low in earnest conversation and in disagreement about how we make such a world.

We sit listening to the storm as it departs, but the rain doesn't touch us here. Lightning slashes through the heavy clouds, but it doesn't bother striking the wilding sea, turns away from the strand, and moves out to sea, at last.

Our quiet talk turns to these Tower times that mark this era. Our voices are gentle, our tone thoughtful. These years of the falling Tower have strengthened and humbled us. Decades of our lives have been spent watching the collapse of top-down systems, observing as they fall, pause, and recalibrate for a while, before they resume their descent. We had some expectations early on that stasis would eventually be reached and rebuilding could begin, shaping those wobbly systems into something more resilient, more ethical, more egalitarian.

But that was not to be. The crashing towers, as we know from the number sixteen card in many tarot decks, continued to remind us that we were caught in a time of irrepressible change. We could not avoid it: resilience and survival have been all. We have held our loved ones and our values close to our chests and tried with all our might to avoid the boulders of catastrophe as best we could. We have lost much and some of it was very dear to us. We have said goodbye to reliability and stability and have learned to cross the marshes while avoiding the quicksand. Looking at our personal and cultural histories, we have resettled ourselves, redefined ourselves, re-mothered ourselves.

Time after time, we have bid a grateful farewell to the departing year and looked with relief upon the new one, only to play out the same scene twelve months later.

Thus prepared, our group of sojourners has made its way to the sea and to this womb, where we have compared notes, sung songs, and danced in soft circles as the tide came in. Tonight we will walk into the arms of the sea and into the face of the full Moon. We will be baptized in cold fire and will emerge unconquered, stepping at last into the Mother World we have tranced into being. At least, that is the plan. As the sun sets, we rise and undress ourselves, combing our hair and washing our faces. The storm is long past, and the beach is completely empty of chairs and sunscreen bottles, children and kites.

We make our way from the womb and onto the old sea path. It is strewn with driftwood, sea glass, a nightskyful of shells, mostly broken. The Moon is up and casts her light upon the water, drawing a white ribbon across the sea's surface. This odd little beach holds a secret, and that's why we have come here. On certain nights, in certain seasons, a luminescence in the waves and on the sand sends sparks onto bare feet and shoulders. Turtles come onto the shore to dig holes with their awkward paddles and then turn to lay their eggs, covering them with flaps of sand before returning to the open sea. On this night, we will welcome these shell-mothers, embrace the tiny lights in sea and on sand.

It is time. We stand facing the rising Moon and are very still. Dark shapes soon emerge from the wave and move past us into the sand behind. The sea, with the tide coming in, is too loud for us to hear the digging, but a slow look over our shoulders shows us the ritual of digging, laying, and covering. The turtles will rest for only a little time before returning to the sea.

When we turn back to the flow of the water, we begin to see the tiny sparklings that are on top of and inside the water. Suddenly, the bioluminescence is everywhere, as far up and down the beach as we can see.

One of us steps forward to touch a foot into the water, and the shimmer can be plainly seen in the sand around that foot. We all step forward then, silent, still, and aware of the great mothers so busy behind us. We form a line and take hands as the shimmer covers our feet and shimmies up our legs. Slowly, with reverence and unbelievable delight, we walk into the sea and into the Mother World.

Perceptions

There are worlds within worlds in all the places we've traveled in our time together. There is above and below. There is here and there. Inside and out. All of these can be and often must be traversed to get a full and helpful picture of where we actually are in time and space but also in history and myth. So many roads and pathways, all of them leading somewhere in this persistent search for the Divines in Their own realms and for the freedom we crave and require from the crushing weight of patriarchal systems and their dangerous attendants.

Chapter 16
The Mycelia Way

The most recent sojourn has brought us here to the open mouth of an earth womb where we wait, again. So much of our journeying is about discerning when to bide and when to move, and patience and endurance are powerful teachers. We are also resting and refreshing ourselves with food and with sleep—another valuable lesson on these open roads.

Those simple pleasures are much needed because our longing to connect with the Mother Tree will manifest in an unexpected side quest that may very nearly derail us. We will realize it isn't a side quest at all. It is the missing puzzle piece that will lead us to this cave as the tide approaches and the storm beckons a world of change.

The Journey

On our way here, to the mouth of the cave, we come across a place of meadow and woodland, some parts of it cleared by our ancestors long ago. The grassy fields are kept trimmed and free of baby trees by the black deer that forage the woodland. There is always a cooling breeze here, and a brook of sweet water runs along one edge of the meadowland, its origin an outcrop of rocks and its path skirting the edge of grass before veering off into the woods.

We have ostensibly come here in search of the Old Mother Tree, a plant that sounds mysterious but is, in fact, a stately old white oak that has stood its ground for centuries. It is surrounded by its offspring, whom it has nursed through fire and lightning. We believe there is much to learn from being in the presence of such a venerable being, and we understand there are flushes of rare and beautiful fungi along the way.

It is tempting to feel a lightness in contemplating such a pleasant journey. But we know better than that. We long to spread our arms around this place and allow the eagerness we feel to drink in the sanctity of the place to carry us into this encounter. A small part of each of us is wary, as experience has taught us.

We arrive in the early morning. The sun has risen but is not yet well up above the woodland, and we remark on the shadows that squirm and dance along the edges of the place. As is our custom, we walk around to get a feel for the spirit—and the spirits—here and discover a flat stone near the source of the brook that bears signs of having been a table for offerings. Remembering our extraordinary welcome at Old Water, we bow three times to the water and leave offerings of food and silver rings on the flat stone. Our cupped hands bring the cold water to our lips, and we drink it down, then pat the coolness of it onto our faces and the backs of our necks.

A sort of sandy area near the edge of the trees draws our eyes—it seems an odd sort of soil for so rich a climate. Wandering to it, we see that it marks an opening between the trees, so that seems a logical place to begin. We can see the Old Mother Tree from the clearing—she is towering over the crowns of her companions—so we know which way to go.

It is not a particularly dense woodland, and it feels healthy and vibrant. There are scurryings as we pass, and the usual citizens of the place go to ground—squirrels, chipmunks, a small green snake. The birdsong is bright, with much variation. We say the names of those we know, but there are unfamiliar voices here, too. A brown thrasher clicks at us from her perch, and we hear her warning, knowing her nest must be close by.

We are not far in when we spot the first fungus, though we have been traveling the mycelia network in one form or another since the very start of our time together. This is the magic carpet of folktales, the road to the everlasting, the way both forward and back. The first flush of mushrooms we see are a soft purple and prolific. Small caps rising on slender necks, so many of them clustered together that we can't possibly count them all.

The next ones we spot are yellow and ruffled, and we know them mainly from brunch. The sweet chanterelles are easy to spot and delicious, alone or in company. Someone speaks their name and a general sigh of omelets past escapes our lips. We laugh when the next is the red and white toadstool of childhood and a mushroom we have always been warned of—*Amanita muscaria*. These ones are so bright—they have the classic fat red cap with bright white nodules—and we stand for some time entranced by their beauty as well as their deadly reputation. They seem to be speaking to us, asking us to come closer. We do and now we are a human ring surrounding a stout growth of these lovely things. We step closer and closer, peering in, listening, under the spell of this magic fungus. One of us suddenly sees another flush of them farther on, off the little pathway, and we instinctively move toward it, aware that we are being called from our destination but feel unwilling to leave the trail of amanitas.

We do the same as before, circling this new batch, listening to them, smelling the slightly fishy aroma that drifts up to our noses. Another group, further on still, compels us to follow. But we are lured away by the discovery of a bouquet of chicken of the woods festooning a stump. Amanitas forgotten for the moment, we walk to the stump. These are dramatic and touchable. We shyly brush fingertips across their orange tips, and a smell of damp soil rises to our noses. These fat chickens have broken the spell of those red caps, allowing us to ramble back to the winding trail that leads us to the Old Mother Oak.

Our path is now lined with peculiar fungi that are folk beings. There are turkey tail mushrooms that fan out like the feathers of great owls. Creepy fungi wriggle along our way. Some look like little penises, others like the fingers of dead people reaching up. The mycelium network is a moving highway, tempting us, always tempting. Brilliant white ones that look like those buttons we get from the grocery store stand sentinel, but they are not the innocents we cheerfully sauté—they are called destroying angel, and we want so badly to step over to the slight mound where they stand so starkly in contrast with the dark greens and browns of the woods. We begin to drift that way, forgetting the lesson of the amanita.

We are pulled back to the chosen path once more and begin to discuss what we are observing. The poisonous ones have a powerful draw on our senses, always pulling us from the road. The medicinal fungi grab us back and set us where we need to be. Surely we are imagining all this? Why would the mycelium world care what direction we traveled, which destination we choose? Again and again, we tested this idea, following the squishy false morels, flat ones the color of autumn pumpkins, and spiky gray ones that advertise their toxicity.

Each time, we are pulled back by the broad fans of medicinal fungi, gently tugging at us, for we have an appointment that we want so much to keep. Despite the distractions, we arrive at last at the base of the Old Mother Oak. Her trunk is quite broad, and she is surrounded by her grown children. There are larger trees in the world and there are older trees, certainly. But this Mother Oak has been waiting for us, calmly going about the business of homesteading the forest, peopling it with her children and with all the other plants that depend on the canopy and the fall's leaves to thrive in a place of mottled light.

If we were given to fantasy, we might think of her as holding court. She is a sacred being, a powerful healing force that nurtures as well as nourishes. We understand why she has come to be called a mother tree as she stands with her gnarled and broken limbs stretched out like arms, patiently waiting for her mobile children to come home.

Her trunk easily endures our repeated hugging and bark-petting until we finally sit on the acorn-strewn ground to lean on her. We can look directly up the trunk to the crown, and we could climb all the way to the top if we could reach the first branch fifteen feet about our heads. Instead we sit and gaze upward, noticing the dead limbs and broken branches that will come down in the winds of the coming winter.

For now the green of the leaves is still true, though some edges are beginning to turn in the cool night air. In a month they will be the color of flame, and then they will remain stubbornly affixed to the branches until the growth buds reactivate in the spring, when they will finally let go and the wood will be silent enough to hear them drop onto their branch-mates.

The bark is rough against our backs, and we are so quiet that the birds begin to sing again. There's a rabbit on the path who must have followed us on the way in. We are so quiet, mostly because we are unsure what happens next. We can feel the waves of healing that ooze out from the old bark. It is a tangible thing, like water from a tap or the dark soil that nourishes our gardens at home.

We feel it then, for the first time in our long pilgrimage—the longing for a home, for the home we left so far behind us. We suspect some of us will finish this journey and return, wiser, better equipped to be the mother trees for our families and our communities. But most of us can never go back to those places that bound us to our fear and to servitude. We will carry the feral church we have sought throughout, carry it in our hearts, marked on our souls and psyches. We have met and continue to meet the Goddesses of these wild places—Goddesses that are strong beyond all reckoning and also tender.

This fine old Mother is a resting place, for now, but the showy, deadly mushrooms have caught our eye again and we become restless in this sadness for a home that never really was. The home-place for us is one we carry with us in our hearts and on our backs. The dangers we face taste of iron, blood, and death. They also taste of adventure, connection, and freedom. In this moment, we are engulfed in the sweet and the salty of knowing, and the ecstasy and the pain of being.

We voice almost none of this as we lean against the Mother Oak. We feel the knowledge flow up from our experiences and into us from the soil and the bark. We are content, though the amanita calls us and we must go.

Perceptions

Throughout our journeys, there have been moments of uncertainty, of danger, but this trickery of the mycelia is one we need to absorb. It is a simple thing to assign mischief or even malice to these strange beings.

But is that the case? It is more a matter of showing each of us the power of nature and the complexities of this Mother World. This invites us to consider human complexities and how these complicated and ancient systems can and should move in interlocking circles to be the connecting point of the Divines—these ancient Mothers—with all of us. In journey after journey, we seek a place of such connection: a feral church of ecstasy and wisdom.

We have touched so much of land and sea, of sky and fire, as we walk between the holy solstice seasons. Our walk has taken us weaving into and out of lives and lands where we have found the mosaic that is the church, the holy vessel of connection and desire. Between forest and sand, we have sought the narrow way, the stony way, the way to which we have been called, trusting (mostly) that the Divines and our intuition would not lead us too far astray. The pleasure we have enjoyed, the terror that has threatened to devour us—both extremes are nothing compared to the luminescence of this holy communion. We give thanks. We give thanks.

Chapter 17
SEVEN NIGHTS BEFORE SOLSTICE

Dear companions on the journey, we are nearly there. We have traveled the breadth and length of the year to arrive again at the gateway to a new season. We stand at the doorway to the possible, and there is much to see, much to learn, much to absorb from this internal and external journey. This next place sits high above the world we know. It is the realm of the Primal Ancestors and contains the matrix of all we are and all we can be.

THE JOURNEY

It is a few days before the solstice, and an excitement has attached itself to our exhausted band of sojourners. In the ever-growing darkness, hunger and fear have given way to enervation. We travel now to greet the morning sun on the solstice. The way is not long, but it is steep. A vantage point sits high on these mountains, a place from which we can observe the brightening of the world without anything obstructing our view. Our earlier visioning of the soon-to-be Mother World has brought us here, crossing this vast plain, looking up to the peaks of the Three Mothers.

The mountains that we call the Three Mothers are not on any maps. You can't book a luxury, all-expenses-paid trip to be a tourist there. There are no trendy cafés or yoga studios. No guide can rent a bus and fill it with eager pilgrims, no matter how spiritual they may be or seem to be. There's no road, for one thing.

The Three Mothers reach into the thin air and perch in one of the liminal places of the world. Ley lines stretch out in all directions from these frosty peaks—lines that connect to Olduvai, Angkor Wat, Baikal, Uluru, Serpent Mound, and so many others.

The Three Mothers lie in between the material world and the realms of spirits. Like old Brigadoon, they can only be found at the edges of space and the ends of time. They glimmer mirage-like before us, the colors of their flanks changing with the wind and the shifting light. We have a ways to go and should make a move.

Be careful in this long grass—biting and stinging insects for sure, as well as the occasional snake or vole. If we stay close together, we should be fine. Relatively speaking.

After all we have encountered since that first solstice, the seemingly never-ending walk across this steppe is only tedious, which is why we are encouraged to tread with caution. The peaks grow larger as we walk, poking our walking sticks into the edges of the tangled grass. The walkers in the front aren't following a designated path. They are simply moving toward that fixed point on the horizon as quickly as they can. We follow the flattened grasses from their passage.

We are quiet now, quieter than usual. Someone softly whistles a familiar song, but none pick up the tune to sing it aloud. There is only the small swishing sound of trampled weeds and sticks used as tools.

At long last, we arrive at the foothills of this range, where boulders lie fallen from the old mountains. We come to stand in a rough circle, facing inward. We look at our feet, our hands—anything but the way up the mountains. In spite of everything, we sit, finding seats on boulders or braving the few patches of naked earth. Water is shared and fruits are passed from hand to hand in a carved bowl.

The sweetness of the fruit, the refreshment of water, and the relief of having come to this final challenge—all these have a profound and surprising effect. We gaze into each other's faces and our eyes crinkle up in the far corners as we smile our first smiles in ever such a long time. The smiles move over our faces until the edges of our lips turn up, too. We share a look of astonishment. How is it possible to be happy in this place, at this time? We have no idea what waits for us at the end of this tangled journey.

We have spilled our guts on the rancid ground, we have tasted death upon our tongues. We have fought, wept, cursed, and kept moving forward. Mile by miserable mile, we have encountered a divine and terrible being who has humbled us, taught us, tended our emotional and physical wounds, and set us free.

We have seen the face of God and She is mother, sister, grandmother, lover, and queen. She has called us again and again, chided us when we wanted to stop, when we had had too much. At every step and in each moment of this wild year, we have come to know that the vast universe is Her Body, and we are a part of that Mystery. Free, feral.

As one, we rise to our feet and reach our hands to each other. Then we move through the last of the boulders and, still hand in hand, begin to climb.

The Three Mothers have names, and each name has come down to us as a simplified, understandable version of the great powers we are now ascending. They are Nemesis, Khione, and Marena. Those names were whispered down the ley lines, the words chanted by our oldest ancestors, beings so far in the past that we no longer consider Them the same species as modern humans. Khione and Nemesis: those names ended up in Thrace and Hellas, and Marena's name wound its way to the thick woodlands of the Ural Mountains.

The Hellenes gave the word *Khione* to their Goddess of cold weather and of death, a Goddess born of rape and grief. For those people, cold and death felt synonymous, and the name seems best spoken through clenched or chattering teeth.

Nemesis is perhaps the name we know best. The word-hungry Hellenes heard that word slashing through the storm and gave it to their awful Goddess of holy retribution, justice flung against any who insult the gods through their hubris.

Marena, She of many names, walks throughout the forested slopes of the northern Ural Mountains, where the shouted words of the Three Mothers were caught in an eagle's nest.

The Slavs know Her as a death bringer who paces the hills, Her apron full of poppets. Her step herds the glaciers and calls down the avalanche.

Make no mistake, these old giants tread Their lands throughout the seasons, as They have done throughout the millennia. They happily share Their names with the land, and the land welcomes Their heavy, confident steps. There is magic here, the oldest and most compelling. It is the magic of plates pushing together and land rising. It is the magic of gales changing the face of the land, of floods sweeping away filth and bringing fertility, it is the magic of fire that burns all it touches. It is not sentimental magic, not the sweet longing of mother for child or lover for lover. This magic is swift and implacable, and it is the life force of these old primitive Mothers who birth everything around Them, destroy it in its time, and then birth it all again.

Our little party of wanderers has a vague notion of all this, which brings us some fear, some anxiety, and not a little yearning. We all feel we have been to this place before, and we breathlessly discuss that as we help each other up the narrow and steep staircase. Some of us are sure we dreamed it. Others remember the feel of the rock under their hands—rock that has been smoothed by cautious pilgrims over many centuries. We speculate on what we will discover when we reach the top, if we ever do. But we are growing increasingly breathless, whether from exertion or altitude it is hard to determine.

When we mounted the staircase, there were alpine flowers in the cracks of the rock as we climbed. But they soon gave way to moss and lichen, and the lichens are changing as we ascend. A moment's pause to catch our breath and to peer upward also affords a chance to look down and study the lichens in their splendor. They are so small, hardly noticeable, but when we take a moment to get our faces close to them, we find a world within worlds. Their colors are sometimes subtle, sometimes garish. Some are soft like forest moss, but most are heavily textured. There are clusters of lichens that seem to have been colonized by other lichens and by mosses.

This tiny world implores us to bide a while and learn more, to discuss the far world with them since we are mobile, and they adhere to their stony perches. But the top of the mountain seems almost close now and we are anxious to conclude this long sojourn. We touch the lichens gently and continue to navigate the steps.

We are grateful to reach the summit before the inevitable fog settles onto the mountain top. The arrival is abrupt, a surprise. Throwing ourselves onto the plateau, we rest a bit and consider the place around us. Some of us lie down. Others are sitting up and peering around. It is a surprisingly broad place, and near one edge there are great stones arranged around a central hearth. If they are natural, they don't look it—they bear a striking resemblance to standing stones we have seen in so many places. These are fashioned into seats with low backs.

Curious, we walk over to this gathering place, for that is what it must be. The coals from the hearth are still warm to the touch, and there is a pile of sticks and branches near one of the chairs. We add some kindling to the coals and soon have a bright fire in the circle of stones. The seats are larger than human size, and some of us struggle to sit in them, like children at the grown-ups' table. A few choose instead to sit on the ground and use the seat as a back support.

The stories begin in earnest then, now that we have recovered from the scary climb. The best part of enduring the frightening, surviving what at first seems unsurviveable, is the tales that grow from the experience. These tales are not, strictly speaking, reports of historic occurrence, for they are as embroidered as a tablecloth and told with panache. Our tales are much the same, and each adds their own remembrance of the city street or the time under water or the beings we met in the desert. Ha! Such embroidery, such perfect truth! We are laughing and interrupting each other as the legends of this time together are woven into garments of life and personal history.

We don't notice that we are not alone. Amid the laughter and shouting, beings have joined us, partially visible but mostly fog. The laughter dwindles away as we feel them near us. At first glance, they are the long-expected fog settling onto the plateau. They move with the same fluid motion, filling in the areas all around us. But there is something unfoglike as they settle near the stone seats and start to assume a loose form.

They are larger than we are but hardly giants. We immediately understand that we have taken their seats and scramble off, standing awkwardly to the side. These fog-mothers are more corporeal now, but not much, as they settle into the chairs and bend toward the little fire.

There have been so many beings in our time together, but there is something about these that puts us at ease. We sit at the side of the seat nearest us and watch the fire, too. After some time, a shift ripples the fog bank, and we see a stone arch in the fire, and on that hob is a clay vessel, much used. It is then we smell the cooking smells. There is the welcome smell of warm bread and stew. Our attention is captured and we realize how hungry we are. The clay vessel is passed between our hosts and pauses at each one of us, and we understand that we are welcome to share in this meal. We do, with gratitude.

Round and round the circle it goes until we are all full. Then it resumes its place on the hob and is replenished from within. In the days that follow, it is refilled again and again. We are never hungry nor thirsty, and when it is time to sleep, we find soft nests behind the seats and we sleep, dreamless, only to wake in the morning to breakfast smells and refreshment.

The fog-mothers gather more form as the days roll on, but they are never entirely solid. They are forever perched on their hard seats, and we suspect they sit in their own counsel while we sleep. When we wake and break our fast, there is more they teach us, more they want to know from and about us.

Our pilgrimage is intimately known to them, and they marvel at the journey we have made to find them, these Primal Mothers. We understand that they laid these paths at our feet and were best pleased when we chose our own way and learned that lesson in a thoroughly unexpected way.

And so those brief days pass in more learning and in delight. On our final evening, the fire is very low and no more kindling is available. As we sit beside the stone seats for the last time, all the fog-mothers but one flow out of their near-physical form, and the fog flows over the edge of the plateau and into the night.

The remaining one has more form than we have witnessed until now, and She stands us in front of Her, one by one. We feel strong hands on our shoulders and an almost electric charge runs through us. This last Primal Mother gives to us Her power, Her strength, Her imprimatur, and Her benediction. When each has been thus blessed, we come to stand at the stone seat nearest the edge of the plateau, so that the one standing before the Mother has privacy in the blessing, in the transfer of power. At last we are all standing together once more, gazing out and up into this night only days before solstice morning, the last night, the first morning.

Night. Cloudless, moonless, starless night. A darkness so profound that our eyes are useless and so dense that our listening ears are useless, too. The nothingness of where we stand is absolute, and within it we feel the grains of ourselves draining away into the void, into the everlastingness of this eternal night. The last of the fog-mothers has flowed into the darkness.

We enter the womb of the Mystery now. Our sojourn to find Her—to know Them—has brought us here at last to the intimate knowledge of Her Mystery, She who is both the Universe and the thing that powers it. She who is. She who was. She who is perpetual, ever moving, ever present.

Finally, we are no longer bound by time or space, for we have entered the ultimate knowing, we have found our feral church. As the individual cells of our being drop away in tiny cascades, we feel the brief touch of each of our comrades on this brave escape. We whisper to each other, and it is the only sound in the enormity of this place. The single words form a kind of patchwork as they float past us.

Yes.

Love.

Free.

And last of all, as we feel the edge of the plateau crumble under our feet, a soft and final

Ahhh

as we slip with unimaginable joy into the womb of time.

She is here. We are here.

We are one.

Perceptions

There are lands all over the earth that are neither here nor there, sitting between time and place. They are most easily accessed through dreams and trance work. Even daydreams can plant our feet firmly in these sometime-places. They can be visited for the sake of experiencing the rarified nature of a land that is not land or water that isn't water. But pilgrimages to these places are most beneficial when we cross the borderlands with a purpose in mind and go, not as tourists to a strange and possibly forbidden place, but as potential immigrants exploring a possible new homeland.

Chapter 18
THE CEREMONIAL RETURN: THE GREAT ROAD AT AVEBURY

The pilgrim road has ended in Avebury. Here we will have a chance to have a hot bath, a change of clothes, and some hours of reflection. Though our journeying has ended here—except for our individual trips home—we now have the privilege to celebrate what we have learned about feral churches and the Mother World and to honor our year of travel in a ritual of celebration and of birth.

THE JOURNEY

We have spent the last three days in Marlborough, sharing rooms at a large bed-and-breakfast place. The inn has a long history and the beds are firm. We spend the first day wandering aimlessly around the town. We eat sausage rolls and drink pints of good local ale. Several of us choose to spend the day soaking in a tub of hot water while drinking mineral water—hydrating on the inside and the outside. Our skin begins to pump up then, and we no longer look dry and haunted. We speak little and think less. The broad processing has not yet begun, but we are all gathering our strength to consider it. Rest is first and then medical attention where needed, mostly abrasions and bruises. There is a twisted ankle and a sprained wrist among us, and these will take a little longer to heal. Poultices have been applied and clean bandages firmly wrapped around.

The first night we sleep so deeply that we have no dreams. None. The second night the nightmares begin, and we decide to sleep in shifts and with a partner. At breakfast the next morning, we hesitate to share what we have seen in the dream world. Each one of us, though, had a similarly themed nightmare. We return home alone, and when we open our front door, everything is the same. The neighborhoods, the cities, the countryside are just as we had left them. Chameleon-like, we all change to fit in, to be back where we were—once again bound, cold, lost in spiritual and emotional agony. It is this horror that brings us awake screaming, and it is this night of fever that we recount over buttered toast and poached eggs the next morning.

The dreams were all so similar that we find ourselves telling each other's nightmares. *And then I unlocked the door to find there wasn't even a layer of dust on the piano...or...for some reason, I was taking a bus home and it traveled through my town and everything—even the people on the sidewalks—was frozen...*

After all we have seen and done, this is so ridiculous that we begin giggling, and the giggles turn into big belly laughs. We pound our hands on the table and laugh so hard that our host leaves her Aga cooker and rushes in to see if we need more tea.

It is at that breakfast that we know not only has the processing begun, but we had been processing all along the journey. We are exactly the people who had begun this thing so long ago, but we have peeled off layers of acculturation all along the way. We arrived here completely naked (in every way except physically—though our clothes were quite ragged) to this old inn in Marlborough. On our final day and night here, we have one more sojourn, and we are ready.

After that breakfast, we put on our pilgrim's clothes and prepare for a longish walk to a local landmark. There we plan to sing down the sun on this old world before moving on to the Red Lion on the next day and taking the processional avenue to Silbury Hill. The end of our quest and the beginning of the new world we are creating.

We have backpacks heavy with sandwiches, thermoses of tea, and packets of ginger cream cookies, courtesy of our kind host. We set off with a hand-drawn map and some general directions. After so many strange lands, these softly rolling hills are quite pleasant to walk along. We end up taking a bus partway and are glad of that. It leaves us near a small, empty carpark and shortens our walk considerably.

The gravel path takes us through pastureland and ends at a gate with a warning sign about the bull. We look at each other and reckon we will risk it. We stay near the fence in case we have to go quickly over or through, with a snorting bull as our motivator. The hand-drawn map proves to be accurate, and we see ahead of us a solitary clump of large sarsen stones, knee-deep in grass and brambles. Leaving the safety of the fence and seeing no bull in sight, we make our way toward the Devil's Den.

We immediately decide that "the Devil's Den" needs a new name. Our host had told us it was the remnant of an old, long barrow, part of the general Avebury cluster of ancient monuments. Most of the stones had been removed long ago, and this leaning trilithon is all that's left. It was also dismantled and re-erected about a century ago. We can see old blobs of cement that once held it in place, but gravity seems to be doing much of that work now.

We sit in our customary crescent, facing the monument—while keeping an eye out for the bull. We take out some food and have a light meal. We discuss the legend of the place, the reason we have come in the first place, as this is a late addition to our time here. As we eat and come into an accord with the place and the stones, we notice how the stones form a portal, a gateway, which seemed fitting. One of us tells the story of its ridiculous name and weaves for us the legend of the large dog with red eyes that is said to haunt the area. We are unsure if the "beast" was ghost or cryptid, but the symbolism is unmistakable.

We are sitting at a yoni-shaped portal from which a red-eyed monster is said to emerge, flowing forth into a pasture where a bull is kept. We rename it the Place of Deliverance and place food at the base of the stones to feed the land spirits and honor the reemergence of the Primal Mothers. Here is a shrine for the Mother World that holds the promise of birth and deliverance.

We settle in nearer the fence in full view of the stones and wait for sunset. As the sun creeps its way down the western sky, we sit quietly, holding the power of that place and matching it with our own power. We hold our hands out to the stones and let our gratitude for all they had been and all they will be flow out from us. We eat a little more as the sky starts to dull into the gloaming.

Then we rise, facing the last streaks of the fiery West and we hold the old world in our arms, in grace and affection. One voice rises first in a light sweet ballad, and each of us joins our voices into that one. As the sun falls ever lower, we sing a funeral song for the old world, and some voices are lifted in a hair-raising keening for all that is lost, all that was stolen, all that was destroyed.

As the twilight settles around us, we sing lullabies to the new world being birthed, and when we are ready, we kiss the Place of Deliverance, pour the last of the wine for all who had gone before, and head back to the fence at the edge of the pasture. Our phones and flashlights come out. Our packs are lighter for the long walk back, and we soon find the gravel path. We come to the car park and start the long walk back to the crossroads where we hope to catch the evening bus back to Marlborough.

We have not walked very far when we hear it coming, mount the steps, and ride back in quiet happiness. A new world. And so it is.

We bid a genuinely fond farewell to our host the next morning, and she has packed us some food for the road, though Avebury is not far away. We take the bus into this little hamlet set in the center of a great henge, and we check into the last inn of this pilgrimage, the Red Lion.

We have the Red Lion Inn to ourselves—that was prearranged by us and for us. There are not throngs of tourists in the Great Henge, and the people of the town have either shut themselves in for the day and night or have taken the bus to the next village or gone into Bath for some shopping. They have been very gracious, and most are excited about these old magics returning to the area.

Since the beginning of the stone-raising and the ditch clearing, this has been a site of ceremony and old power. That humans have grown so comfortable with this great machine of the Goddess is both curious and comforting. Tales of walking spirits abound here, and to walk the processional way is to walk with the oldest Citizens and the spirits they served.

It is quiet but for the crows and the bleat of lambs. The parish church, St. James, is silent—no bells will be rung today, for the rector is in his study, drinking bourbon and reading Pelagius.

We are settled in and have taken clean, new garments from our clothes cupboards—another bit of foresight. We won't get dressed just yet, though—we have chosen another old tradition to bring into the Mother World.

In our travels, we heard stories of warriors returning from battle in the far past. One story concerns a magical stick that is wrapped with strips of fabric, usually from the clothing of ancestors or heroes. This implement was carried by warrior bands for several reasons. It was a talisman of the people left behind, for whom they were fighting. It also carried the strength and wisdom of the collective and held the power of generations. The stick served as a reference point for the band much as flags function in later centuries. They symbolically brought all those forces to bear so that their place in their family and community was not forgotten. Soldiers in more modern times carry pictures of their sweethearts and families, either printed or on their phones, for the same reason—to remember why the hardships, the injuries, and the deaths are deemed necessary: a sacred notion of protecting and preserving the precious land, the homeland.

When these warriors returned to their village, they were greeted outside the confines of the village by their families and the elders. They were thanked for their work and for keeping the people safe. The dead were taken to a special place to rest on the grass of their native soil before their funerary rites commenced.

The warriors were stripped of their weaponry, assured that each piece would be lovingly tended, cleaned, sharpened. Then the families and the rest of the people departed to do that promised work, leaving only the old women, the grandmothers and the old aunties.

Their filthy, gore-stained clothing was taken from them, and the old women bathed the warriors in fresh water, trimmed and untangled hair and beards, dressed wounds, served warm tea. They were wrapped in woven cloth and made to rest. After a time, each soldier was bathed in milk, rinsed with water, and given back their workaday clothes to symbolize their return to the people, as the people.

Mindful that we are bringing back to modern memory some of the lost and powerful parts of our older history, we have chosen to do both things. We spend time in the early afternoon wrapping special fabric pieces onto strong sticks. There are bits of dried pond weed, a ribbon from the mane of the pack horses, a hank of bison hair, and more things that we have gathered along the way. Each talisman is different, reflecting the unique perspective of each of us. We marvel at the things each has kept and tell stories, reminiscing about those people or that place. The sticks are laid beside our new clothes, and we go to make ourselves ready for the final—and also the first—ritual.

We bathe each other in milk, and our skin is rubbed with almond oil. The tangles are combed or cut out of our hair, and our nails are trimmed to a reasonable length. Both fingers and toes have smooth edges now, safe edges, strong edges. We smell better than we have in a very long time, but a part of us longs for the scent of pine forests and wood smoke.

We have decided to assemble in the courtyard outside the inn and go from there to the lych-gate to begin the procession. We tuck our ancestor sticks into our belts and thank the landlord for his hospitality, reminding him we will be out very late. He assures us he will hear us when we get back and will be waiting with hot coffee and sticky rolls.

There are torches leaning against the lych-gate, waiting. We walk slowly over to the torches and each take one up. They are not lit yet. We will carry them along the processional way and light them as the Moon rises over Silbury Hill.

Silbury Hill is a peculiar place, but we all agree we are being called to it. It is ancient—as is everything in Wiltshire, including the buses—and is a portion of an enormous ceremonial complex whose earliest monuments were raised during the Neolithic. It is not surmounted by a stone circle nor earth works. There is a big hole in the top where an eighteenth-century shaft collapsed fairly recently. It is simply a human-made hill and looks like a soft breast on the body of this dear land.

We set out, walking in pairs—two by two, like the animals going to the Ark. And isn't that just what we are doing? Walking away from the despairing and dissolving old world and walking up the firm gangplank onto the ship that will carry us to safety, post deluge?

Our step is unhurried and we walk in silence. The sun is lowering, as we had intended, since we want to arrive in near darkness at our destination, our destiny. The stones stretch long shadows across the sere grass. The ravens at the low hill are calling the family in to the night's roost, and other birds are having their last chat before the night falls. Then it is the owl's time and the nightingale's.

The grass is soft beneath our feet, and we are once again grateful for the gentle, aged rolling of these downs. This processional way has been walked countless times and is well-signposted. No fear of getting lost, though at this point in our pilgrimage, there is little that we fear. We have stepped from our sojourner roles and walk now with the confidence of the ages, as wisdom-keepers, as the descendants of powerful ancestors and the kindred of the Primal Mothers. We are judges and leaders, here to reveal and uphold a world both ancient and perfectly new.

The path rises gently, with standing stones at intervals, marking the way. We admire the textures and the variation in shapes and sizes. There are faces there in the near-twilight: deeply etched, they are as animated as our own. One eye open, the other shut. A gaping and toothless mouth sits below squinting eyes. Our animist hearts recognize these stone people, and we nod to them as we pass. When we reach the top of the incline, we come to stand in our usual crescent in front of the sentinel stone. We look around at each other—our hair flowing back from our scratched, bruised, and happy faces. All at once, we bow to this sentinel. Once, twice, three times. A band of crows flies over our heads, heading west. But we turn again to the east and reassemble our procession to Silbury Hill.

The sun is nearly down now and our shadows precede us. We are following a direct trail—heralded by an elderly signpost—away from Wayland's Smithy. Another hill to climb and this is another pasture, though the cows have all gone home this late in the day. There is a cloutie tree to our right, and we stop to honor the prayers and wishes that it holds. Two of us unwrap strips of fabric from around the torch, and we speak our own prayers and intentions as we tie them on. As we turn from the tree, we see the faint glow of the full Moon beginning her ascent.

At our current pace, we are still a good twenty minutes from our destination, but we are in no hurry. How could we rush through this last step, after the twists and turns of our quest for this feral church? Time had stood still, it had run free, it had sent us fleeing down Plumb-Killt Woman's mountain, it had pushed us into the maenads' dance. Here time flows out from us as we walk, and our road wends into the future, with the vivacity of the present and the power of the past. Everywhere are signs of the Primal Mothers, each blade of bent grass is our church, each stone and tree is the altar upon which we sacrifice what must be sacrificed to make this Mother World.

To think of sacrifice is a delicate thing, filled with momentary grace and a frisson of old fear. As we make our way down the other side of the hill, the Moon shows her forehead, and we remember all that we carry with us—and all that we leave behind.

We stretch out now, no longer walking in pairs but as a broad line. Because of our torches, we cannot walk hand in hand, so we walk with our shoulders as close together as we possibly can. Sometimes a hand stretches lightly over a neighboring shoulder or a head leans in to rest for a brief instant on a companion's upper arm.

We have come directly across the grass and now stand at the base of this breast that lies upon the land, this old Silbury Hill. We can't see the Moon yet, for she is rising behind the hill. She will reveal herself soon enough, and we have a few things to prepare before that moment.

The firelighters are ready for the torches and we once more gather close together, touching each other lightly, nodding both thanks and encouragement. There are tears, of course, but there have been plenty of those along the way. Each of us takes out the small stick that we carry in remembrance of all we are, all we've done, and all we have yet to do. We stand together one last time and carefully light our torches. We hear a nightjar calling in the brush, with its strange mechanical song. As we step away from each other, mindful of the torches, the ticking song continues. But it stops when we have come to our positions for moonrise.

Our voices have been unused for much of the day, and when we begin to sing, we are croaky as the nightjar and have to clear our throats. We begin again, a song we have chosen for this liminal moment. We sang the old world to sleep yesterday with a lullaby at the Place of Deliverance. Tonight we will celebrate this birth, this rebirth, with songs of joy and triumph.

The nightjar begins again, as we sing, and we hear an owl from behind us. We lift the torches and ancestral sticks high, as the Moon seats herself on the top of the breast of Silbury. Our voices are raised in Schiller's ecstatic poem, set to Beethoven's equally ecstatic Ninth Symphony, the final movement, the "Ode to Joy."

> *Ancient Goddess, Joy,*
> *We greet thee, daughter of Elysium!*
> *Wild we dance into your temple,*
> *Drunk with fire and love for thee*
> *Ancient magic binds together*
> *What the times would tear apart.*
> *Hand in hand, we all are kindred*
> *In the glory of your heart.*

We sing it until our voices are gravel and the Moon has continued her flight into the night sky. Our torches have burnt themselves out, one by one, and we tuck our ancestor sticks back into our belts.

The birthing has been so long and the need is so profound, but it is done. This new world, this Mother World, will need care and tending as all new things do. Many, many more voices are needed to raise the holy songs. Many, many more hands are needed to build new places, new systems, new ways of being in kinship with all of this glorious baby world.

But it has begun. This is the feral church we longed for, this land, this place, this interlocking and sacred system that we call Earth, that we call home. There is much to do in this Mother World. There are seeds of all sorts to save and to plant. There are nourishing plants to tend and harvest in due time as well as invasive vines that will choke out the young trees if we don't tend them diligently. We have wandered long in the wild and learned how we fit into the ways of desert, of sea, of stone and mountain. We are at home, at last, in the whole of our Terra Mater—the wild lands and the tended ones—because we are bound in the double helix of the Goddess, of life, and of our collective future.

At this moment, a barn owl shrieks her wild and mournful call, and a nightingale begins to sing.

Now She is everywhere.

Now She is everything.

Postlude

The end of this pathworking is also the beginning of new roads and undiscovered country: we step from the feral churches we have discovered and into our free lives. These churches require no tithing for upkeep, no fundraisers for the new roof, no cattle call for well-heeled worshippers. Feral churches stand in the lost and forgotten places, those in the world and in our souls. Our journey now is to find the ones nearest our hearth and home—the old city park, the quiet cemetery, the last bit of old-growth forest, the wild river. We find them when we sit at the bedside of the dying, diaper the new child, drink tea with a hopeless friend, plant a garden in a food desert. We are finding feral churches and their concomitant fierce ministries everywhere, for the need is great.

In all those places, in every place, we find Her waiting. She is the ancient Matrix of all that is, this Primal Mother who birthed us and was torn from us on the riptide of history. In Her vast body and Her never-ending soul we have come to find inspiration, understanding, altars upon stone and tree and broken heart. To call one of Her sacred names is to know Her in this modern, trauma-sparked world, ancient and forever.

Go now. All that we need, all the power that is, lies beneath our feet and within our hearts. Follow the roots, follow your roots. May your prayer be the howl of wolf, the shriek of panther, the unearthly scream of the north wind. May you dance and heal in Her name and in your own. Take the power and save what can be saved.

Appendix
Feral Resources

A Glossary of Feral Places

In writing this book, I have traveled in my imagination to places that hold a resemblance to places I know or have known. But they are transformed into liminal places of challenge and of power and magic.

The Bookshop of the Ancient Mothers

One interpretation of those mysterious Akashic Records. I've used my imagination to conjure such a place in the mountain settings of home, and the shop itself owes much to my many years as a bookseller.

The Hollow Hill

A plain, near a meadow. As a lifelong mountain resident, I have always been intrigued by the concept of hollow hills. This one is the embodiment of my work with the spirit beings I refer to as the Good Neighbors.

THE MOTHER TREE
An actual type of tree. These mother trees exist in many forests and function as only good mothers do—to produce, protect, and nourish their offspring. The mushrooms in that canny wood are based on the mushroom people that have appeared in my dreams since childhood.

THE THREE MOTHERS
The Three Mothers walk between the worlds of spirit and matter. They are Goddesses and also mountains, spirits of the place as well as the place itself. The names are familiar to many of us, and the idea that they hold the power of the planet and send pulses of energy throughout the ley lines of the world felt right.

THE MYCELIA WAY
This concept reflects our current knowledge of the expansive nature of the fungal world with which we share the planet. Mushrooms—which are only one expression of fungi—play a significant part in the world's folklore traditions. It is used here to remind the reader of the profound and quite literal connection of all things in the biosphere. These mycelia also represent the idea of the Prankster, a being who challenges and changes the direction of lives.

THE OLD WATER

The pond on the steppes. It stands in for all those places where we don't fit in but endeavor to learn the lessons of the situation and make the best of the encounter.

THE PLACE OF DELIVERANCE

The name given to the Devil's Den, which is an actual place near Marlborough, in Wiltshire. I wanted a vision for the sojourners that linked past to future and took away the fear and shame around "the devil" in order to repurpose this old monument for the Mother World.

THE RED LION INN

A real place, situated in the town of Avebury. It dates from 1802 and boasts an indoor well and a thatched roof. It is mostly a pub, with very good food and ale. Visit www.chefandbrewer.com.

SILBURY HILL

A human-constructed mound that was erected in about 2400 BCE, in what is called the late Neolithic age. It is part of the ancient civil parish of Avebury in Wiltshire in the United Kingdom.

The hill's purpose has been speculated on but remains unknown. It is made-up mostly of chalk and was created in many sessions, building the mound higher each time. There have been several excavations of the site, the early ones inspired by tales of treasure, no doubt. One of those earlier tunnels collapsed in 2000, which led to a new exploration using modern equipment. Silbury retains her mystery.

I use it here as a visual for the nurturing breast of the Goddess as Earth. I have been to the site many times, and it never fails to take my breath away in the moment and haunt my dreams for months after. That nourishing place felt like the perfect place to end our long search for the feral church.

ORGANIZATIONS

There are masses of information out there. Some of it is good and some of it is doubtful. As you search for your connection to a feral church, here are a few places I recommend for inspiration about Goddesses, women's spirituality, transforming culture, and living a life filled with the presence and energy of the Primal Mothers.

For more specific information on forming a feral circle, gathering, or church in your community, join the movement at www.feralchurch.org and www.feralchurch.com.

Association for the Study of Women and Mythology, www.womenandmyth.org

Christ, Carol, www.feminismandreligion.com

Dashu, Max, Suppressed Histories Archives, www.suppressed-histories.teachable.com

Divine Feminine App, www.thedfapp.com

Girl God Books, www.thegirlgod.com

Mago, www.magoism.net

Millionth Circle, www.millionthcircle.org

Raine, Lauren, www.laurenraine.com

Tippett, Constance, www.goddesstimeline.com

Wolf, Kaitlin Ilya, www.priestessofcycles.com

Feral Church Playlist

Here is a personal playlist of music that inspires me, comforts me, or gets my heart strong for the work. I offer it here to give you an idea of the music I listened to while pondering the mission of writing this book, as well as what I listened to as I was writing. I generally don't listen to anything with words as I'm writing because the story distracts me. If any of these are new to you and you are curious, they are easily found with an internet search or downloaded through any good music service.

Amanita: *Soul Flight*

Anonymous 4: *An English Ladymass*

Bach, Johann Sebastian: Brandenburg Concertos

The Band Perry: "If I Die Young"

The Beatles: "Let It Be"

Beethoven, Ludwig von: Symphony no. 9, Fourth Movement

Belloni, Alessandra: *Daughter of the Drum*

Bulgarian State Television Female Voice Choir:
  Le Mystère des Voix Bulgare

Dvorak, Antonin: Symphony no. 9, the *New World Symphony*

Fleetwood Mac: "Landslide"

Gabriel, Peter: "Solsbury Hill"

Green, Krista Chapman: "Altars of the Moon," "Fire and the Mountain"

Grieg, Edvard: "In the Hall of the Mountain King"

The HU, feat. Serj Tankian and DL of Bad Wolves: "Black Thunder"

LaMonte, Gina: "Empress Down Rattlesnake Road," "Uvalde Lullaby"

McKennitt, Loreena: "All Souls Night"

Minogue, Áine: "Song of Keening"

Mozart, Wolfgang Amadeus: The Requiem in D minor, K. 626

Mussorgsky, Modest: "The Great Gate of Kiev," *Night on Bald Mountain*

O'Connor, Sinead: "Óró, sé do bheatha abhaile"

Orff, Carl: *Carmina Burana*

Saint-Saëns, Camille: "Danse Macabre"

Sinatra, Frank: "My Way"

Recommended Resources

This is the tip of the iceberg for books on Goddess thealogy. The golden age for this scholarship seems to have passed, so many of these books may be most easily obtained in second-hand bookshops or internet sources.

Barstow, Anne. *Witchcraze: A New History of the European Witch Hunts*. Reprint, San Francisco: HarperOne, 1995.

Berger, Pamela. *Goddess Obscured: Transformation of the Grain Protectress from Goddess to Saint*. London: Robert Hale, 1988.

Blackie, Sharon. *Hagitude: Reimagining the Second Half of Life*. Novato, CA: New World Library, 2022.

Bolen, Jean Shinoda. *Crossing to Avalon: A Woman's Midlife Quest for the Sacred Feminine*. San Francisto: HarperSanFrancisco, 2004.

———. *The Millionth Circle: How to Change Ourselves and the World*. Newbury, MA: Conari Press, 1999.

———. *Urgent Message from Mother: Gather the Women, Save the World*. York Beach, ME: Conari Press, 2008.

Cameron, Anne. *Daughters of Copper Woman*. Madeira Park, BC, Canada: Harbour Publishing, 2002.

Christ, Carol P. *Rebirth of the Goddess: Finding Meaning in Feminist Spirituality*. Milton Park, Oxfordshire, UK: Routledge, 1998.

Christ, Carol P., and Judith Plaskow, eds. *Womanspirit Rising: A Feminist Reader on Religion*. San Francisco: Harper and Row, 1979.

Daly, Mary. *Beyond God the Father: Toward a Philosophy of Women's Liberation*. Boston: Beacon Press, 1973. Reprint, 1993.

Dames, Michael. *The Silbury Treasure: The Great Goddess Rediscovered*. London: Thames and Hudson, 1976.

Dashu, Max. *Witches and Pagans: Women in European Folk Religion, 700–1100*. San Francisco: Veleda Press, 2017.

De Shong Meador, Betty. *Inanna, Lady of Largest Heart: Poems of the Sumerian High Priestess Enheduanna*. Austin: University of Texas Press, 2000.

Diamant, Anita. *The Red Tent*. London: Picador Books, 2007.

Ehrenreich, Barbara, and Deirdre English. *Witches, Midwives, and Nurses: A History of Women Healers*. New York: The Feminist Press at the City University of New York, 1993. Reprint, 2010.

Eisler, Riane. *The Chalice and the Blade.* San Francisco: Harper and Row, 1987.

Endicott, Gwendolyn. *The Spinning Wheel: The Art of Mythmaking.* Portland, OR: Attic Press, 1994.

Erdrich, Louise. *Antelope Woman.* New York: Harper Perennial, 2016.

Estés, Clarissa Pinkola. *Untie the Strong Woman: Blessed Mother's Immaculate Love for the Wild Soul.* Louisville, CO: Sounds True Publishing, 2013.

Federici, Silvia. *Caliban and the Witch: Women, the Body, and Primitive Accumulation.* New York: Autonomedia, 2004.

Gadon, Elinor W. *The Once and Future Goddess.* Northamptonshire, UK: Aquarian, 1990.

Gage, Matilda Joslyn. *Woman, Church and State: A Historical Account of the Status of Woman through the Christian Ages.* Chicago: Charles H. Kerr & Company, 1893.

Gilligan, Carol. *In a Different Voice: Psychological Theory and Women's Development.* Cambridge, MA: Harvard University Press, 1982.

Gimbutas, Marija. *The Language of the Goddess.* New York: HarperCollins, 1991.

———. *The Living Goddesses.* Edited by Miriam Robbins Dexter. Berkeley: University of California Press, 1999.

Goldsmith, Barbara. *Other Powers: The Age of Suffrage, Spiritualism, and the Scandalous Victoria Woodhull.* New York: Alfred A. Knopf, 1998.

Hurston, Zora Neale. *Tell My Horse: Voodoo and Life in Haiti and Jamaica*. Philadelphia: J. B. Lippincott, 1938.

Jensen, Derrick. *A Language Older Than Words*. White River Junction, VT: Chelsea Green Publishing, 2000.

Kingsolver, Barbara. *Animal, Vegetable, Miracle: One Year of Seasonal Eating*. New York: HarperCollins, 2007.

Kinstler, Clysta. *The Moon Beneath Her Feet*. New York: HarperOne, 1991.

Kramer, Heinrich, and Jacob Sprenger. *The Malleus Maleficarum*. Edited by Montague Summers. Mineola, NY: Dover Publications, 1971.

Lerner, Gerda. *The Creation of Patriarchy*. New York: Oxford University Press, 1986.

Livingstone, Glenys. *A Poiesis of the Creative Cosmos: Celebrating Her with PaGaian Sacred Ceremony*. Bergen, Norway: Girl God Books, 2023.

Magliocco, Sabina. *Witching Culture: Folklore and Neo-Paganism in America*. Philadelphia: University of Pennsylvania Press, 2004.

Monaghan, Patricia. *O Mother Sun! A New View of the Cosmic Feminine*. Freedom, CA: Crossing Press, 1994.

Noble, Vicki. *The Double Goddess: Women Sharing Power*. Rochester, VT: Bear and Company, 2003.

Pollard, Joshua, and Andrew Reynolds. *Avebury: The Biography of a Landscape*. Stroud, UK: Tempus, 2002.

Ranck, Shirley. *Cakes for the Queen of Heaven: An Exploration of Women's Power Past, Present and Future.* East Sussex, UK: Delphi Press, 1995.

Reilly, Patricia Lynn. *A God Who Looks Like Me: Discovering a Woman-Affirming Spirituality.* New York: Ballantine Books, 1996.

Schlain, Leonard. *The Alphabet Versus the Goddess: The Conflict Between Word and Image.* New York: Penguin, 1998.

Silko, Leslie Marmon. *Ceremony.* New York: Penguin Books, 2006.

Simard, Suzanne. *Finding the Mother Tree: Discovering the Wisdom of the Forest.* New York: Vintage Books, 2022.

Sjöö, Monica, and Barbara Mor. *The Great Cosmic Mother: Rediscovering the Religion of the Earth.* San Francisco: Harper and Row, 1987.

Starhawk. *The Earth Path.* San Francisco: New York: HarperCollins, 2004.

_____. *Truth or Dare: Encounters with Power, Authority, and Mystery.* New York: HarperCollins, 1987.

_____. *Webs of Power: Notes from the Global Uprising.* Gabriola Island, BC, Canada: New Society, 2008.

Stone, Merlin. *When God Was a Woman.* Orlando, FL: Harvest/Harcourt Brace, 1976.

Teish, Luisah. *Jambalaya: The Natural Woman's Book of Personal Charms and Practical Rituals.* San Francisco: HarperColllins, 2021.

Thorpe, Adam. *On Silbury Hill*. Beaminster, UK: Little Toller Books, 2014.

Walker, Barbara. *The Crone: Woman of Age, Wisdom and Power*. New York: HarperCollins, 1988.

Ward, Tim. *Savage Breast: One Man's Search for the Goddess*. Hans, UK: O Books, 2006.

Watkins, Alfred. *The Old Straight Track: Its Mounds, Beacons, Moats, Sites, and Mark Stones*. London: Methuen & Co., 1925.

Wolkstein, Diane, and Samuel Noah Kramer. *Inanna, Queen of Heaven and Earth: Her Stories and Hymns from Sumer*. New York: Harper & Row, 1983.

To Write to the Author

If you wish to contact the author or would like more information about this book, please write to the author in care of Llewellyn Worldwide Ltd. and we will forward your request. Both the author and the publisher appreciate hearing from you and learning of your enjoyment of this book and how it has helped you. Llewellyn Worldwide Ltd. cannot guarantee that every letter written to the author can be answered, but all will be forwarded. Please write to:

H. Byron Ballard
℅ Llewellyn Worldwide
2143 Woodale Drive
Woodbury, MN 55125-2989

Please enclose a self-addressed stamped envelope for reply,
or $1.00 to cover costs. If outside the U.S.A., enclose
an international postal reply coupon.

Many of Llewellyn's authors have websites with additional information and resources. For more information, please visit our website at http://www.llewellyn.com.